D0323522

The Literature
of East Germany

The Literature
of East Germany

THEODORE HUEBENER

Frederick Ungar Publishing Co.   *New York*

Copyright © 1970 by Frederick Ungar Publishing Co., Inc.
Printed in the United States of America
Library of Congress Catalog Card Number: 75–114610
International Standard Book Number: 0–8044–2401–2

Contents

Preface

This book is intended as an introduction to a field of literature
which is largely *terra incognita*, not only to the American reader
but also to the German-language reader. In an article in *The
New York Times* in 1967 Rudolf Leonhard, editor and critic of
Die Zeit, wrote: "If one were to ask an average citizen of Hamburg about German literature east of the Elbe, he would probably be able to name no more than two writers."

Even a cursory knowledge of the literature of East Germany
is extremely limited, chiefly because of the West German prejudice against that satellite state and the refusal to accept its political status. Yet a considerable body of literature has been produced since World War II, some of which merits the attention of
the cultured reader as well as that of the professional Germanist.

In any case the study of the literature of any people is of interest.

In an attempt to present the more important writers and their major works a number of problems in terminology arise. The very name of East Germany—Deutsche Demokratische Republik or DDR—is unacceptable to West Germans since it implies political recognition of an independent state. West Germany is officially known as the Bundesrepublik Deutschland or the Federal Republic of Germany. For the sake of brevity and simplicity I have used East Germany for the German Democratic Republic and West Germany for the Federal Republic of Germany.

Another difficulty in terminology is caused by the fact that East Germans use "communism" and "socialism" almost interchangeably, although the latter tends to appear more frequently. I have used both terms. Also, East Germans regularly employ the words "fascist" and "fascism" when referring to National Socialism and the Third Reich. "Nazi" and "National Socialism" rarely occur. I have given preference to Western terminology, usually writing "Nazi" when referring to the policies, acts, and adherents of Hitler.

There is very little West German critical material available at this time. The three most rewarding West German works are *Deutsche Literatur in West und Ost* and *Literarisches Leben in Deutschland* by the critic Marcel Reich-Ranicki, and *Mitteldeutsche Erzähler* by Hans Peter Anderle. (Note the designation *mitteldeutsche* for East German.) Reich-Ranicki discusses eleven East German writers in some detail, at times with rather sharp expressions of opinion. I have quoted him occasionally. Anderle, who is more sympathetic and open-minded, treats twenty-two authors somewhat briefly. Anderle's book is really an anthology of short selections from representative prose works, with rather brief biographical notes on the authors.

The greatest difficulty is encountered in attempting to evaluate East German writings fairly and to express a balanced opinion on their literary merit. West German critics are for the most part unsympathetic or hostile. Reich-Ranicki is quite severe in several instances. Anderle is more charitable. East German critics are quite unreliable. Frequently they laud mediocre writers in panegyric terms, evaluating their works on the basis of the author's devotion to communism rather than his ability to produce a work of literary merit.

The most comprehensive and most recent East German reference work is the volume entitled *Deutsche Literaturgeschichte*, edited by Professor Hans Jürgen Geerdts and published by the Volk und Wissen Volkseigener Verlag in East Berlin in 1965. A corps of specialists is now expanding it into eleven volumes. The present work of 768 pages gives a complete survey of German literature from the beginnings to the present. The opinions expressed about early and medieval German works are generally in agreement with the traditional ones in any Western history of German literature. This cannot be said for the judgments expressed about modern writers, many of which are entirely untenable.

An excessive amount of space is devoted to the writings of Karl Marx, Friedrich Engels, Rosa Luxemburg, and other political leaders, whose works would be mentioned only incidentally, if at all, in any Western history of German literature.

The titles of all the German works mentioned in the text of this book are given in the original German. If an English translation exists, the English title is given within parentheses after the publication date of the German edition. Where no English translation exists, the title appears in quotation marks. All translations of quoted material are mine except where indicated as otherwise.

It is hoped that this brief survey, which is merely an introduction, will lead to further study of the literature of East Germany.

May I express my thanks to my wife, Elizabeth, for her careful reading of the manuscript.

THEODORE HUEBENER

Fairleigh Dickinson University

Form and Content

No body of literature—in fact, no form of art—is an entirely unique and independent creation. It is always a continuation, modification, or transformation of something that preceded it. In view of this, it is reasonable to examine briefly the antecedents of the literature that was produced in East Germany after World War II.

German Socialist Literature before 1945

German socialist literature, then, did not begin with the establishment of the German Democratic Republic. What was written there after 1945 clearly continued leftist-inspired writing of pre-

1

ceding decades. In fact, East German critics claim that the seeds of socialist literature—without being designated thus—appeared in Germany a century or more ago. By that they mean the works of many earlier writers who described the sufferings of the lower classes. Even certain works of Goethe and Schiller are praised for reflecting the struggles of the proletariat.

Although they certainly cannot be claimed as socialists, many German writers of the nineteenth century did occasionally express ideas that the radicals found acceptable, even though there were no clearly marked political implications. There come to mind certain works of such authors as Kaiser, Toller, Werfel, Heinrich Mann, and Gerhart Hauptmann.

East German literary historians assert that the socialist writers of today are merely continuing one of the basic currents of German literature, namely, concern with the worker and the peasant. The East Germans claim not only the more liberal writers of the nineteenth century; they reach way back to the sixteenth century and point to Sebastian Brant, Thomas Murner, and Thomas Münzer as outstanding social critics.

Many German writers of the early 1920s expressed their revulsion of militarism and their sympathy for the misery of the lower classes. The socialist concept of the search for the new man appears in the dramas of Georg Kaiser (1878–1945), especially in *Die Bürger von Calais* (1914; The Citizens of Calais) and in *Gas* (1918). Kaiser's skill in describing the hated capitalist system is praised by the East Germans, but his ignorance of revolutionary ideology and his lack of appreciation of the aims of the proletariat are deplored.

Similarly, Ernst Toller (1893–1939) is praised by the East Germans. Although he was definitely on the side of the workers, he was doubtful of the success of their program. This is reflected in his dramas *Die Wandlung* (1919; The Transfiguration) and *Masse-Mensch* (1921; Mass-Man). In his *Die Maschinenstürmer* (1922; The Machine Wreckers) he does express the hope of a better world for suffering humanity.

Franz Werfel (1890–1945), too, expressed deep feelings of altruism and brotherhood in his prose and poetry. In his finest novel, *Die vierzig Tage des Musa Dagh* (1933; The Forty Days of

Musa Dagh) he describes the heroic resistance of the Armenians against their Turkish oppressors. Although he wrote a highly emotional "Revolutions-Aufruf" (Revolutionary Appeal), he, like Kaiser and Toller, is criticized by the East German literary specialists for lack of understanding of the aims and philosophy of the revolutionary movement.

Gerhart Hauptmann's works are discussed in detail in the official East German history of literature (*Deutsche Literaturgeschichte*). His sympathy with the exploited is praised. Hauptmann, however, firmly rejected any connection with the socialist movement at the court trial that arose over his allegedly subversive drama *Die Weber* (1892; The Weavers). Nevertheless, the East Germans hoped to win him over. Spiritually crushed by the bombing of his beloved Dresden, the octogenarian poet was visited by Johannes Becher, one of the prominent writers of East Germany, in October of 1945 in Agnetendorf. According to Becher, Hauptmann agreed to join forces against the reactionaries for a rebirth of German culture. In the midst of preparations for his relocation in East Berlin, he died on June 6, 1946.

Socialist Writers

It is evident, then, that at the beginning of the twentieth century many German writers, including outstanding and, in most instances, conservative ones, occasionally in their works dealt with the fortunes of the poor and the misery of the oppressed. Even though they sometimes became thoroughly aroused over the defects of society, none of them joined the socialists or were politically active. In fact, as has been pointed out, they showed little understanding of the political and economic implications of the radical labor movement.

There were, however, numerous professing socialist writers, very few of them of first rank, who devoted themselves entirely to the cause of the proletariat. They had accepted what later became a basic thesis of East German ideology: the conviction that literature was one of the most effective means for stirring up the masses and stimulating them to reject capitalism.

A book was an arsenal, a poem a bomb. Brecht expresses it in his "Lob des Lernens" ("praise of learning") :

> Hungry one, seize the book, it is a weapon.
> You must assume the leadership.

At first the socialist writers dealt primarily with the sufferings and struggles of the worker from a purely personal point of view. It was not until 1928 that systematic promotion and direction of the socialist literary movement through party channels was undertaken.

As indicated above, literature was looked upon as a tool, a weapon, which was to serve a practical purpose. It was not merely a form of entertainment or a medium for the esthetic expression of the author's personal thoughts and feelings.

Poetry was found to be particularly effective for inciting to action. Poems were not to be read in the quiet of the home but to be recited, vociferously and with fervor, amid the excitement of noisy political meetings.

As a sample of this type of verse "Gesang der Jungen" ("song of the young") may be cited:

> The future of tomorrow still remains to us,
> We see it boldly and full of hope;
> We will break the old yoke
> Of slavery and build
> For mankind a rich field.
> And even if now in song
> Only the joy of May is heard,
> Get out! Get up! The morrow dawns!
> The mother of freedom is the deed.
> The song shall become truth.

Events of the day were often introduced into this type of poetry, as, for example, the mutiny on the imperial Russian warship Potemkin (1905) in a poem of the same name by Heinrich Kämpchen. The last stanza follows:

> How my heart laughs in my bosom
> That the slave finally broke the chain
> And that he will swing the sword.
> Good luck to you, Potemkin, rebel ship!
> You were the first in the struggle!

Didactic and agitatory poems and songs of this type were nothing new; they had appeared in German literature before 1948. Known as *politisches Lied* (political song) they went back to the time of Heinrich Heine. Famous chiefly for his romantic, sentimental, and humorously ironic verse, his virulent political poems are overlooked. The refrain of "Doktrin" (1844) runs:

> Drum the people out of their sleep,
> Drum reveille with the power of youth.
> March ahead, always drumming,
> That's all there is to it.

In the same year he wrote "the masses no longer bear their earthly misery with Christian patience; they long for happiness on earth. Communism is a natural result of this changed view of life. . . ."

In his macabre poem "Die schlesischen Weber" (The Silesian Weavers) Heine predicted ominously:

> Old Germany, we weave thy shroud,
> We weave into it the threefold curse,
> We weave, we weave.

Another writer of political verse was Ferdinand Freiligrath, who cried:

> Man of work, awake,
> And realize your might!
> All the wheels will stand still,
> If your strong arm wills it.

Many *Arbeiterlieder* (workers' songs) of this type were published. They regularly denounced the Prussian system and praised the communist program.

Out of the *politisches Lied* the first East German lyrics developed. They continued a tradition that had existed for over half a century. A considerable body of this agitatory verse had been written in Germany before 1945. The leading writer in this category was Johannes R. Becher.

Literature in Exile

Some of the radical writers became so extreme in their utterances that they were considered subversive by the authorities of the mildly socialist Weimar Republic. As communists these writers had of course no use for the new democratic German state. A number of them were imprisoned. Willi Bredel, the tireless worker-writer of Hamburg was incarcerated three times—in 1923, 1931, and 1933. Even so distinguished an author as Ludwig Renn, famous for his novel *Krieg* (1928; War) was accused of "literary high treason."

When Hitler came into power in 1933, most of the socialist writers fled from Germany. Some went to Russia, others to France or Switzerland. A number of those who went to the Soviet Union—Willi Bredel, Johannes R. Becher, Erich Weinert, and Friedrich Wolf—founded the National Committee Freies Deutschland, whose purpose was to hasten the collapse of the Nazi regime. They also published a magazine, *Das Wort*.

A number of the writers went to Spain where they fought in the Spanish Civil War. This experience furnished them with rich material, which they made use of in their writings. So many books on the Spanish Civil War appeared that they form a special category in East German literature. The more distinguished novels were: *Grüne Oliven und nackte Berge* (1945; Green Olives and Bare Mountains) by Eduard Claudius, *Die erste Schlacht* (1938; "the first battle") and *Leutnant Bertram* (1944) by Bodo Uhse, "Rosina" (1938) by Alfred Kurella, "Araganda" (1939) by Hans Marchwitza, "Die drei Kühe" (1938; "the three cows") by Egon Erwin Kisch, "Schlaflose Nacht in Barcelona" (1938; "sleepless night in Barcelona") by Erich Weinert, and *Der spanische Krieg* (1955; The Spanish War) by Ludwig Renn.

East German critics considered the books on the Spanish Civil War a valuable contribution to their literature, since, as they claimed, a new phase of the "socialist man" was revealed. Placed face to face with death on the battlefield, the proletarian hero emerged.

Two older West German writers who later went over to the East Germans wrote some of their major works in exile. This is true of Arnold Zweig, who worked on some of the later volumes of the Grischa cycle while in Israel. Anna Seghers fled to France in 1933 and to Mexico in 1940. While in exile she wrote *Der Kopflohn* (1933; A Price on His Head), *Der Weg durch den Februar* (1935; "the way through February"), *Die Rettung* (1937; "the rescue"), *Das siebte Kreuz* (1946; The Seventh Cross), and *Das Ende* (1945; "the end").

The outstanding example, however, is Bertolt Brecht, who wrote some dozen prose works and plays while in exile. These include such major works as *Leben des Galilei* (1943, 1945, 1947; Galileo), *Die Heilige Johanna der Schlachthöfe* (1932; St. Joan of the Stockyards), *Der gute Mensch von Sezuan* (1943; The Good Woman of Setzuan), and *Mutter Courage und ihre Kinder* (1941; Mother Courage and Her Children).

While in Prague Willi Bredel wrote *Die Prüfung* (1934; "the test") and Hans Marchwitza, while in New York, wrote his novel *Die Kumiaks* (1934).

Non-Political Poetry

Many of the East German poets continued the tradition established a century ago of writing verse of a political character. To a lesser extent there is, however, some non-political poetry being produced. The Dutch critic, Ade den Besten, tries to prove this conclusively in the little volume *Deutsche Lyrik auf der anderen Seite* ("German poetry on the other side"), published by the Carl Hanser Verlag in Munich in 1960.

As Ade den Besten points out, there is a great variety in style and theme. Many of the poems are expressionistic or neo-roman-

tic. Most of them express moods, reveries, or reflections. Among
the 125 selections, there is not a single poem with any political
implications. The words "socialism" and "communism" do not
occur. That this type of verse is not approved of by the East
German critics is seen by the fact that of the twenty-four poets
quoted, only seven are mentioned in the official *Deutsche Literaturgeschichte.*

As a sample of the character of the poems in this volume,
"Blühe, blühe mir näher" ("Bloom, bloom closer to me") by
Stephan Hermlin may be quoted:

> Bloom, bloom closer to me,
> Lovely evening face.
> Greet in the departing light
> The observer who is going blind.

> White face. How white
> Under the cold moon
> That dwells in the night,
> Rolling along on starry track.

> Hark, someone is singing in a dream. . .
> Does your frightened mouth
> Weep to me at a late hour
> Under the midnight tree?

> Alas, I am erring greatly
> In the labyrinth of what I've dreamed.
> From what has been neglected
> No one will save us any more.

> Lay your too white hand
> Deadly on my hair.
> The night is swelling wonderfully
> In the sinking land.

> Farther, oh, farther,
> Complaining face.
> Abandon in the dawing light
> Your companion.

Socialist Realism

By the time they had returned from exile, the socialist writers had developed in broad outlines a rather definite pattern for East German literature. Very soon, however, the party leaders took over the control of art and literature to make sure that there would be no serious deviations from communist standards. The basic thesis, formulated by Lenin and reinforced by Ulbricht, was that all cultural efforts were to serve the state.

Since it proudly professes to be "a republic of workers and peasants," it is not strange that the leading topic of literature in East Germany should be the worker and his milieu. He is the hero of the novels and the plays; his problems and difficulties provide the substance of the conflicts and tragedies.

Social realism also requires the action to take place in East Germany. Some aspect of the life of the common people should be portrayed. The hero, the central figure, must be a worker of humble origin, loyal, and clean-living. His fidelity is rewarded; because of his devotion and faithful service he rises in his profession.

A leading character must be a representative of the communist system— a functionary of the party, a higher official, or an officer. He may be pictured as intelligent, competent, and experienced, but preference is to be given to the kindly, humane, and understanding type. Because of his broad vision he is able to smooth out all difficulties.

As a foil to him and to the hero, there is the somewhat weak and vacillating intellectual, who is ultimately won over or eliminated. Representatives of West Germany are regularly portrayed as villains; all capitalists are ruthless exploiters of the proletariat.

Everything is presented as black or white; there are no grays. Political and social problems are presented, but they are all to be solved from the Marxist point of view. Indecision, doubt, and the questioning attitude are taboo; there must be complete and unswerving faith in the communist ideology.

"Socialist realism" was the style of writing proclaimed in

1934 at a meeting of the Soviet League of Authors in Moscow. It is a mixture of political, esthetic, and moral ideas. Writers were enjoined to present "a truthful and historically concrete picture of reality in its revolutionary development." Socialist realism was nominally accepted by East German writers, although the concept was soon subjected to a number of modifications due to practical considerations.

The political leaders and party literary arbiters in East Berlin tried to exert a rigid control over literary production. This was done largely through conferences of authors and publishers, and through the German Academy of Fine Arts. The Ministry of Culture—an office occupied for a time by Johannes R. Becher—also exerted a strong influence on writers and publishers.

The rigidity of the control has, however, not been constant. So far there have been three rather well defined periods in the literary and artistic development of East Germany. At first there was the attempt to force socialist realism on all writers as the solely acceptable norm. This was not entirely successful and gradually faded out, or was modified.

The second period began with the so-called "thaw" of 1956–57, when the severity of censorship was somewhat relaxed. Through a conference of authors and publishers at Bitterfeld in 1959, a second cultural level was established. A movement was begun to encourage gifted workers to write. To help them, staffs of editorial workers and readers were set up. The results were moderate, but at least a more liberal literary climate was created.

The "thaw" (*Tauwetter*), which was recognized by the conference of 1959, was formally accepted by a second conference at Bitterfeld in 1964. More liberal standards for writers were established. The ideal of linking literature with practical work experience was announced. Professional writers were to go into industry, and workers who felt so inclined were to write. Outstanding examples of the writer-worker are Willi Bredel, Hans Marchwitza, and Erwin Strittmatter. A classic case is that of Christa Wolf, who entered a "work-brigade" of a railroad car factory and suffered an accident. She makes use of this episode in her novel *Der geteilte Himmel* (1963; The Divided Sky).

East German Critics

In accord with the criteria set up, the task of the official critic is to encourage writers who promote propaganda and to attack those who deviate from the party line. The basic themes of literature are not universal problems of human existence, but rather the various kinds of politico-social phenomena. The worker stands in the center; not the worker in general, but the member of a given trade or branch of industry. This has led to a curious development. Novels have appeared that are concerned with the chemist, the cabinet-maker, the miner, the dairyman, the peasant, etc.

The tight critical straitjacket has kept most of the East German critics in line, but occasionally an impatient voice, annoyed at the dull, hard dogmatism of socialist criteria, speaks out. Thus Wolfgang Joho in *Sonntag* of March 26, 1961, wrote:

A cancer of our literary criticism, which often makes it so sterile and its reading so boring, is the lack of a point of view (*Standpunktlosigkeit*) of our critics. . . . So often we experience the fact that the critic accepts the opinion of the official censor. . . . One would like to know what the critic thinks of the book. One learns nothing. Does he have a point of view? We assume he does. Unfortunately, he does not have the courage to express it.

Only the writer who expresses the ideals of the party is considered sincere. With reference to the integrity of an author, Erhard John, Director of the Section for Esthetics of the Institute for Philosophy at the Karl Marx University in Leipzig, writes:

Honest is the artist, the writer, or philosopher who says and writes what he thinks. We greet the honesty of those who have recognized the great truth of our age, the historic mission of the working class, and the natural development of socialist reconstruction, who endeavor to portray it artistically and to show that the working class accepts everything great and valuable that mankind has so far developed culturally, taking it in hand, cultivating it, and developing it further.

In other words the writer is honest only if he presents the party point of view; if he espouses any other, he is dishonest. The mission of the writer is solely to spread the ideals of the party by artistic means.

Clear evidence that the East German critics judge on the basis of politics and not literary ability is presented in the *Deutsches Schriftstellerlexikon von den Anfängen bis zur Gegenwart* (Volksverlag: Weimar, 1960). About 750 German authors are treated; half of the articles are on writers of this century. They are grouped in various categories; the two major divisions being "socialist" and "bourgeois." Authors outside East Germany are arbitrarily classified as bourgeois, but they are subdivided into "bourgeois-anti-fascist," "bourgeois-humanist," and plain "bourgeois." Various West German authors with a social message are put into these categories. Only one gets the highest designation, namely, Günther Weisenborn.

The *Lexikon* discusses many German authors who have treated social questions, such as Gerhart Hauptmann, Wilhelm Raabe, and Karl Kraus. They are praised for revealing the wretchedness of social conditions; they are rebuked for not accepting the socialist solution. This grouping includes Büchner, Hebbel, Goethe, and Schiller. *Wilhelm Tell* and *Faust* receive high praise, but their authors are put in the bourgeois category.

East German authors, on the other hand, are given fulsome praise. Johannes Becher is lauded as the outstanding representative of "socialist German national literature" and "the greatest German lyricist" of our times. Erwin Strittmatter's modest literary efforts are termed a "brilliant" artistic achievement. Willi Bredel has rendered "an everlasting service" to socialist German national literature. Stefan Heym's novels are "breathtaking and gripping." Hans Marchwitza is "a towering genius who stands as a high example to numerous younger socialist writers."

West German critics must smile when they read such statements. Fantastic as many of the opinions are, the volume cannot be ignored. It is the sole literary reference work in East Germany available to librarians, writers, publishers, and teachers.

Although the party literary dictators have exercised rather rigid control, not all writers have submitted supinely to their dictates. Some have gotten away with a good deal; others have been arbitrarily suppressed. A classic case is that of the popular lyric poet and ballad singer, Wolf Biermann. At first he enjoyed great confidence, being even permitted to sing before West German audiences. In 1966, however, he was forbidden to publish his works or to sing in public. He is not even mentioned in the *Deutsche Literaturgeschichte*. This is one of the favorite methods of dealing with refractory authors; they are simply relegated to oblivion.

Even outstanding writers have had difficulties with the Central Committee. Bertolt Brecht had serious quarrels, and sometimes had to make drastic changes in his plays. Erwin Strittmatter's *Ole Bienkopp* (1963) was frowned upon officially because the progressive hero of the novel opposes the reactionary bureaucrats and reveals their ineptness. Christa Wolf, too, has faced hostile elements in the party but has stood her ground. Her controversial *Der geteilte Himmel* went through a dozen editions.

Recent Trends

Despite the fact that until 1945 the two Germanys were one country with the same historic development, the same institutions, and the same language, the intellectual as well as political estrangement has been sharp. As pointed out previously, East German literature has been deliberately ignored in West Germany, or treated with disdain and derogation.

Even reference by name to the Eastern Zone has been studiously avoided. East Germany is officially known and shown on the West German maps as *Mitteldeutschland*, on the theory that "East Germany" is the former Reich terrain now occupied by Poland. In newspapers and magazines one reads *Ostdeutschland, die russische Zone, die Ostzone, "da drüben"* (over there), and *"zwischen Elbe und Oder"* (between the Elbe and the Oder). Its official name, Deutsche Demokratische Republik, is not used. In print a concession is sometimes made by putting *"DDR"* in quotation marks, or by referring to it as "the so-called *DDR*."

Very few books by East German authors have been published in West Germany (e.g., Arnold Zweig, Anna Seghers, Johannes Bobrowski). In one case it took two years until a noted novel (Strittmatter's *Ole Bienkopp,* 1963–65) was issued by a West German firm. Publishers are hostile; so are critics. The general attitude is: How can there be any artistic creativity if art and literature serve the state? Ordinary human problems and individual development must be ignored in favor of a glorification of communism. This of course is true only in part. Some East German authors have produced works of merit, even though the problems and the point of view are different from those of the West.

East German literature is definitely a part of German literature, just as that of Austria and Switzerland is. Due primarily to the change in political policy, a more friendly attitude toward the cultural activities of East Germany has developed recently in West Germany. More and more East German books are being published west of the Elbe. Leading newspapers, such as the *Frankfurter Allgemeine Zeitung,* and magazines, such as *Die Zeit,* often publish articles about East German literature.

Interesting is the change in attitude toward Brecht. In the 1950's a performance of one of his plays was likely to provoke protest and controversy. Now his dramas are not only popular with the general West German public but also form an important part of the required reading in the secondary schools.

The liberal West German writers' league, Gruppe 47, established contacts with East German authors. Bobrowski, for example, was invited to read at one of the meetings of the group. In fact, he was awarded a prize. After 1966, however, these contacts declined again for a while because of pressures from the more reactionary authorities of East Germany who want to maintain what they call *"eigene sozialistische DDR-Kultur,"* i.e., an independent socialist East German culture.

East German writers, besides Brecht, who have found favor with the West German public are Anna Seghers, Arnold Zweig, Johannes Becher, Johannes Bobrowski, and Peter Hacks. Two novels that have been widely read are Christa Wolf's *Der geteilte Himmel* and Hermann Kant's *Die Aula* (1964). The East German film version of Christa Wolf's novel was shown in West German motion picture theaters and on television.

Wolfgang Biermann's collection of verse *Die Drahtharfe* (1965; "the wire harp") was published only in West Germany, since he had become *persona non grata* in East Germany. There he is completely ignored; he is not mentioned in official literary reference works. He now lives in West Germany.

It was only natural that those writers who were born and brought up in West Germany and who had gone through two world wars should show a preference for writing about the Reich, the Nazi terror, and World War II. These were the events and situations with which they were most familiar. The communist literary arbiters did not rule out such works, although they indicated repeatedly that too much time and attention should not be devoted to the past. They wanted books that presented a favorable picture of life in the new socialist state.

Some writers have tried to combine the old with the new, as for instance, Dieter Noll in his novel *Die Abenteuer des Werner Holt* (1960; "the adventures of Werner Holt"). This first part describes the hero's career in the war; the second part (*Roman einer Heimkehr*, 1963; "novel of a return home") brings him home and introduces him to the problems of civilian life.

On the whole, the younger generation, that is, those born after 1920, are occupying themselves with portrayals of life in East Germany. A considerable variety of background is depicted —the large urban plant, the little village, and the fishing hamlet at the seashore. Romance, too, enters in. The critics have no objection to this, as long as it does not stress erotic elements. These are frowned upon as characteristics of the decadent and corrupt capitalist West. In general, too, the portrayals of persons have become more natural and convincing; the older black and white stereotype has disappeared. Judging by the latest publications, one may say that East German writers are trying to develop a literature that is distinctly their own.

The Writers
and Their Works

The bonds between West and East German literature are close; they are physical and personal, as well as historical. A number of the more distinguished East German writers grew up and achieved their earliest successes in the older united Germany, long before there was any thought of a German Democratic Republic. Later they left their homeland and moved to East Germany, in many cases after several years in exile.

As examples, four outstanding writers of East Germany may be named. They are Arnold Zweig, Anna Seghers, Ludwig Renn, and Bertolt Brecht. Zweig wrote his first novel in 1911, and his fame was established by *Der Streit um den Sergeanten Grischa* in 1927. Anna Segher's *Das siebte Kreuz* appeared in 1942, in English. *Krieg*, by Ludwig Renn, was published in 1928, the same year as

Remarque's *Im Westen nichts Neues* (All Quiet on the Western Front) . Also, in the same year, Bertolt Brecht's *Die Dreigroschenoper* began its triumphant march across the stages of Europe and America.

The pre-1945 contribution of Zweig, Seghers, Renn, and Brecht to West German literature is unquestioned. What they have written, however, since their retreat into the communist camp is not highly regarded in the West. It is interesting to examine their literary production in East Germany and to note what changes have taken place in their style and in their ideas.

Many lesser East German writers—for example, Bredel, Uhse, Claudius, Strittmatter, Heym, and Becher—began their literary careers in West Germany. They produced their major works, however, after they had crossed the Elbe.

Arnold Zweig   (1887–1968)

Of the German novelists who migrated to East Berlin after 1945 the dean and the best known was Arnold Zweig, the author of *Der Streit um den Sergeanten Grischa*, whose literary activity extended well over half a century. In West Germany he was generally regarded as a writer of the past who had outlived his fame. In East Germany, however, he is read, commented on, and widely used as the theme of dissertations in university seminars. West of the Elbe he is occasionally denounced; east of the Elbe he is idolized. Unfortunately, the false judgments pronounced on him are due solely to political and ideological considerations. After all, it was only at the close of World War II, when he was already over sixty, that he went over to the communists. He died in 1968.

Arnold Zweig, born on November 10, 1887, in Glogau, Lower Silesia, was the son of a merchant. For seven years he studied German literature, philosophy, and the history of art at several German universities. He began to write early; even as a student he published poems, dramas, and short stories.

Obviously under the influence of Thomas Mann's *Buddenbrooks* he wrote the chronicle of the decline of a Jewish family, entitled *Aufzeichnungen über eine Familie Klopfer* (Notes on a

Family Klopfer) in 1911. A year later he wrote his first successful original work, entitled *Novellen um Claudia* (Claudia), which is an impressionistic psychological study of two young lovers. The same couple, Claudia and Walter, reappear thirty years later in the novel *Das Beil von Wandsbek* (1947; The Axe of Wandsbek), but the circumstances are entirely changed.

In his first drama, *Abigail und Nabal* (1913), Zweig placed the action in an Old Testament setting. In the drama *Ritualmord in Ungarn* (1914; Ritual Murder in Hungary) he treated the problem of anti-Semitism.

Zweig was deeply devoted to the German classical writers, especially to Lessing, Wieland, Schiller, Goethe, Kleist, and Heine. His favorite was Kleist. Zweig said Kleist's play *Der Prinz von Homburg*, which symbolizes the Prussian ideal, was the most beautiful of the German dramas.

Corresponding to his enthusiasm for Kleist was his attachment to the philosophy of Kant. Some of Kant's basic ideas as well as Hegel's demand for morality and justice are predominant in Zweig's novels. Zweig was imbued with idealistic philosophy, the German classics, and the Jewish spirit.[1]

These were not merely intellectual aspects of Zweig's character; he also acted according to them. When World War I broke out he identified himself unhesitatingly with imperial Germany. To him it represented Kant's categorical imperative and Hegel's ideal state. Other writers protested against the war, but not Zweig, the Prussian. He entered the army in 1915 and fulfilled his military duties loyally, serving in France, Serbia, Hungary, and (for 13 months) at Verdun.

In 1917 he was assigned to the press bureau of the high command in Kaunas. His experiences on the eastern front brought about a complete change in his outlook on life. He said later, in 1956, that he "had gone into the First World War as a conservative idealist and individualist and had come home as a champion of the rights of man and a better structure of society." Deeply impressed by the horrors and the sufferings he witnessed, he decided that in the name of reason and humanity a repetition of such a holocaust must be prevented. Militarism had to be combated. He had become a pacifist.

In this new spirit he wrote a drama, *Das Spiel um den Sergeanten Grischa* ("the play about Sergeant Grischa"), which he completed in 1921. It was a failure; no one would publish it or produce it.

In addition to his thoughts about the war, Zweig was preoccupied with the plight of the millions of Eastern Jews, which he had witnessed with his own eyes. He became convinced that the only solution was the founding of a Jewish national state in Palestine, the ancient homeland of the Jews. Zweig had become not only a convinced pacifist but also an ardent Zionist. These two vital traits of his character have been consistently ignored in the biographical sketches appearing in East Germany, for communism has no use for either pacifism or Zionism. In fact, a number of facets of his personality were difficult for communists to accept.

Zweig's origin, education, and mental and spiritual development were quite bourgeois. What characterized him, however, was not his middle-class attitudes but rather his Jewishness. Zweig devoted his best years not to communism but to Zionism. In fact, it seems rather strange that he should have opted for East Berlin after World War II.

Even as a small child he felt the hostile pressures of the outside world. An anti-Semitic ordinance compelled his father to give up his business in Glogau and to move to Kattowitz. He lost his faith in Jehovah but not his faith in his *Judentum*.

His Jewishness is quite different from that of other Jewish writers for whom it was frequently a burden and a problem (cf. Heinrich Heine). Free from all religious connotations, his Jewishness is something perfectly natural, rational, and acceptable to him. It produced neither *Weltschmerz* nor melancholy; it was neither a curse nor a blessing.

Zweig, however, was also a loyal Prussian. He confronted Prussianism with a Jewish spirit and Jewishness with a Prussian ethic. He had the Jewish confidence in the ethical power of reason and the confidence of the Prussian in the moral effectiveness of order.[2] He was never nervous and temperamental; he was always self-possessed and calm. There is no unrest or divisiveness in his novels; they maintain an atmosphere of equanimity and harmony. Zweig was not aggressive but mildly conciliatory. What he said about the Jews is neither apology nor caricature; he neither glorifies nor attacks. He describes phenomena, classifies them, and interprets them. He handled his problems through the media of the essayist, the dramatist, and the novelist.

During the years of the Weimar Republic, Zweig wrote extensively about the Jews and Zionism, contributing many articles to newspapers and professional journals. In his novels, too—for example, *De Vriendt kehrt heim* (1932; De Vriendt Goes Home) and *Junge Frau von 1914* (1931; Young Woman of 1914), and even later in *Der Streit um den Sergeanten Grischa* (1927; The Case of Sergeant Grischa)—Jews play major roles. Zweig in these years was frequently denounced as a "fanatical Zionist and nationalist Jew."

His attitude toward communism at that time was definitely critical and unfriendly. Together with forty-one other German intellectuals, including Albert Einstein and Heinrich Mann, he signed, in 1930, a protest against the execution of a number of specialists in Russia. Later he wrote, "The dictatorship of the proletariat is abhorrent to me like any dictatorship. . . . The idea of a new order of society is being taken care of very badly in Russia." It was not until 1952 that Zweig visited Russia and saw the Soviet system with his own eyes. He had acquainted himself with the writings of Marx, Engels, and Lenin, and their influence is evident in his later novels, although only in a general and superficial way. He was far more deeply influenced by the psychoanalytic theories of Freud. This appears in his *Novellen um Claudia* and in many of his later works.

The unsuccessful drama *Das Spiel um den Sergeanten Grischa* was transformed into the novel *Der Streit um den Sergeanten Grischa* and became a world success. Since this famous book is so typical of Zweig and is his *magnum opus*, it may not be amiss to briefly relate the plot.

While the German command in 1917 was quietly consolidating its hold on Poland after driving back the Russians, a friendly spirit grew up between the German soldiers and their prisoners. Among the prisoners was a certain Sergeant Grischa who was the foreman of a labor gang. While loading a freight car on a siding he secretly left a small tunnel in the lumber where he concealed himself one night. The train left the next morning and kept going for four days toward the south. When it stopped Grischa crept out and wandered through the countryside. He joined a group of refugees who had taken shelter for the winter in a wooden building and lived with Babka, gray-haired but still young. In the spring the refugees disbanded. For safety's sake Babka gave Grischa the identification tag of a dead Russian soldier. He assumed the name and role of Sergeant Bjuscheff, a deserter allegedly trying to get back to the Russian lines.

In his wanderings Grischa reached Mervinsk, where the Germans had established headquarters. Considerable rivalry prevailed there between the army under the command of General von Lychow and the military police under General Schieffenzahn.

Discovered by the military police Grischa was put on trial, accused of being a spy. Condemned to death, Grischa broke down and confessed that he was not Bjuscheff the deserter, but Grischa an escaped prisoner.

Ponsanski, a Jewish lawyer impressed by Grischa's story, brought the facts before General von Lychow. Two guards from Grischa's prisoner camp identified him, and Ponsanski demanded that the decision of the court-martial be set aside.

Schieffenzahn, however, ordered Grischa's execution within twenty-four hours. Upon von Lychow's vigorous protest, a reprieve was sent by telegraph, but because of a heavy snowstorm, the telegram was never delivered.

Despite the fact that Grischa finally realized that he would be executed, he poured the poisoned brandy that Babka had brought to poison the guards down the drain. He was shot after digging his own grave. His child was born just after his death. The case of Sergeant Grischa was closed.

Eight further volumes followed, which form the so-called Grischa cycle. There were *Junge Frau von 1914, Erziehung vor Verdun* (1935; Education before Verdun), and *Einsetzung eines Königs* (1937; The Crowning of a King). The action of these novels takes place during World War I. The various characters—soldiers, officers, prisoners, and nurses—are transformed by their experiences. They are confused, misled, instructed, and trained by the war. The war dominates their thoughts, their feelings, their conversation, and their dreams. The war makes them wiser, tougher, and more cruel; it is a test of endurance. The earlier novels of the cycle were still written in the style of *Der Streit um den Sergeanten Grischa,* but none can compare with it. The novels written after 1945 are all boringly subservient to the communist line.

Despite the fact that Zweig was greatly influenced by Thomas Mann, he was not obsessed with the depressing moods of that writer. He was intrigued with life, he observed it, loved it, and enjoyed it. His world was secular and rational, clear and comprehensible.

In his Grischa cycle the problem of the conflict between the individual and the state stands in the foreground. Zweig condemns militarism, shows the senselessness of war, and portrays a comprehensive cross-section of society. *Der Streit um den Sergeanten Grischa* became immensely popular; within three years it was translated into ten languages. It did not appear in the Soveit Union until 1938, eleven years after its original publication.

After the Nazis had driven him out, Zweig fled as a convinced Zionist to Palestine (1933). Several of the later volumes of the Grischa cycle were begun there. He was rather content in Haifa, for he lived in a German enclave. When the new state of Israel was established, he was deeply disappointed. As he had fought German nationalism in the Weimar Republic, he fought Jewish nationalism in Palestine. At the same time he tried to promote better understanding of Germany and combated the hatred felt for the Germans in a series of articles entitled "Antigermanismus." It was quite evident that he was fundamentally a German.[3]

While in Haifa he wrote *Das Beil von Wandsbek* (1943; The Axe of Wandsbek), in which he described the German scene critically and benevolently, censuring and defending. It is the story of a Hamburg butcher who, in 1937, takes over the role of the official hangman and executes four condemned anti-Nazis. He is ostracized by most of his fellow townsmen and finally commits suicide—the innocent burger becomes a guilty man. The protagonist is both executioner and victim. Although Zweig skillfully portrays the psychological reactions of the average citizen under a dictatorship, he fails completely in giving a true picture of life in the Third Reich. The book was considered so un-Marxian that Zweig was compelled to add an epilogue, set in Palestine, in which the Soviet Union is held up as the spiritual home of all who fight Nazism.

In May of 1948 the Republic of Israel was founded; in October of the same year Zweig arrived in East Berlin. He remarked: "Ich kann nur in einem deutschen Sprachmilieu leben . . ." [4] (I can live only in a German-language milieu). During his Palestinian exile he had paradoxically come to the conclusion that he was first and foremost a German writer. The East Germans were eager to win this distinguished author to their cause and wooed him. Zweig accepted their invitation and settled in East Berlin. Why he did so, is still somewhat of a mystery.

He had never felt quite at home—not in imperial Germany, nor in the Weimar Republic, nor in Palestine. He was old, ill, tired, and almost blind. In East Germany, however, his prestige was unquestioned; here at last he might feel as if he had a real home. And so he apparently rationalized that he was a member of the just state of which he had dreamed since his youth. He reveals himself, almost autobiographically in his novel *Traum ist teuer* (1962; Dream Is Dear). The hero remarks significantly: "Even a slow current finally tires the swimmer."

Just as the heroes of his novels are almost always ready to make compromises, so Zweig adjusted himself to the rigid demands of the communist state. He accepted the severe censorship, which excludes two of his most cherished ideals, i.e., Zionism and Freudianism. The restrictive forces are not just general matters of principle but are expressed in very concrete practices. The author is provided with "assigned readers" and "cooperative editors."

An endeavor has been made to bring some of Zweig's former novels into line with communist ideology. One such novel is *Die Feuerpause* (1954; The Firing Pause), the basis of which is his 1930 novel *Erziehung vor Verdun* (Education before Verdun). These efforts have not been very successful. Even East German critics have been disappointed by the result. The same attempt was made in the case of *Die Zeit ist reif* (1957; The Time Is Ripe), which is based on *Junge Frau von 1914*. The communist ideas that are introduced do not fit in smoothly and give the book a schizophrenic character. Instead of being a denunciation of imperialistic war and the decadence of bourgeois society, and a paen to the achievements of socialism, *Die Zeit ist reif* portrays a nostalgic farewell to the pleasures of prewar Europe and to better times when the individual was still an individual.

The same can be said of all of Zweig's later novels written in East Germany. His attempts to satisfy the socialist critics were at times pathetic. In *Traum ist teuer,* for instance, it is evident that Zweig simply could not detach himself from some of his earlier ideals. Reminiscent of Sergeant Grischa, a young Greek sergeant who has slapped a fascist officer is prosecuted by the British. His life is finally saved by a Jewish psychoanalyst from Berlin, Karthaus, who is the real hero of the novel. Although the British are pictured as humane and decent, Karthaus turns his back on them and becomes a communist. He also rejects the ideal of a Jewish national state. The story is spoiled by the political ideas that are forced upon the reader.

Summarizing Zweig's career, then, it may be said that his belief that in East Berlin he would find a favorable milieu for the completion of his literary endeavors was a great mistake. After 1948 his reputation declined and his skill deteriorated. His fame will rest on what he wrote before 1948. He will remain the author of the superb novel about Sergeant Grischa.

Friedrich Wolf   (1888–1953)

Next to Brecht, the East Germans consider Friedrich Wolf their outstanding dramatist. His major plays are: *Professor Mamlock* (1934), *Floridsdorf* (1935), *Das trojanische Pferd* (1936; "the Trojan horse"), *Das Schiff auf der Donau* (1938; "the ship on the Danube"), *Beaumarchais* (1940), *Patrioten* (1942; "patriots"), *Dr. Lilli Wanner* (1944), and *Was der Mensch säet . . .* (1945; "what man sows . . .").

Wolf also enjoyed fame as a novelist. His most popular novels are: *Zwei an der Grenze* (1938; "two at the frontier"),

Sieben Kämpfer vor Moskau (1942; "seven fighters before Moscow"), *Der Russenpelz* (1943; "the Russian fur"), and *Heimkehr der Söhne* (1944; "return home of the sons").

Friedrich Wolf, of middle-class origin, sailed the seven seas as
a sailor in his youth. Later he studied art and medicine. During
World War I he was a ship doctor. In 1927 he joined the Communist Party and became a member of the League of Proletarian
Revolutionary Writers. Forced to flee in 1933, he went to the
Soviet Union. On his way to Spain to fight in the Civil War, he
was arrested in France and interned in the camp Le Vernet from
1939 to 1941. While there he wrote his play *Beaumarchais*. Upon
his release he again went to Russia, where he was active as a
lecturer among the German soldiers in the prison camps. In 1945
he went to East Germany. For a time he served as the East German ambassador in Warsaw.

In both his novels and his plays Wolf stressed the restoration
of the dignity of man.

In *Professor Mamlock* the main character is a physician and
scholar who has made notable contributions to science. He is
vigorously opposed to National Socialism, but as an intellectual
he cannot rise to positive action. Relying on the traditional hu-
manistic ideals of bourgeois society, he is confident that decency
and justice will ultimately triumph. A noble-minded individual,
he is crushed by the ruthless forces of Nazism.

In *Das trojanische Pferd* Wolf portrays the heroism of youthful underground fighters in Germany, and in *Patrioten* the struggle of the French resistance to the Nazi terror. In *Beaumarchais*
Wolf depicts the indecisive and wavering attitude of the liberal
intellectual who fails to join the revolution. Wolf's plays proved
popular not only in East Germany but also in the Soviet Union,
where *Das trojanische Pferd* was especially successful.

Friedrich Wolf was one of the first socialist writers to return
to German soil in 1945. He heartily endorsed the communist
point of view that the theater was a rostrum from which to preach
the ideals of the revolution and that the drama had a didactic,
educational (propagandistic) task to perform. In his essay "Das
Drama als Waffe und Werkzeug" (1949; "the drama as weapon
and tool"), Wolf wrote:

Art as the weapon against those ever of yesterday (*die ewig Gestrigen*) is a specific function of the drama. But the drama is also at the same time an important tool—a tool for the building of a new world. . . . On the ruins of the old, we are today building the new. We build new insights, new human beings, new dwellings, new enterprises—an entirely new life!

In his dramas *Was der Mensch säet* . . . and *Wie Tiere des Waldes* (1947; "like animals of the woods"), he stresses the devastating evils of National Socialism. In the play *Bürgermeister Anna* (1950; "Mayor Anna") he discusses political and social problems of East Germany. A colorful picture is presented of the struggles of a woman mayor against prejudice and tradition in a small village.

The East German critics have highly acclaimed Wolf's historic tragedy entitled *Thomas Müntzer, der Mann mit der Regenbogenfahne* (1953; "Thomas Müntzer, the man with the rainbow banner"). The sixteenth-century religious radical is portrayed as the able leader of the revolting peasants.

Wolf is highly esteemed in East Germany not only for his plays but also for his practical contributions to the creation of "the new German theater . . . which became a rostrum for the presentation of a new socialistic Germany."

Ludwig Renn (born 1889)

Of the many books written about World War I, the three most distinguished ones in German were Zweig's *Der Streit um den Sergeanten Grischa* (1927; The Case of Sergeant Grischa), Erich Maria Remarque's *Im Westen nichts Neues,* and Ludwig Renn's *Krieg* (1928; War).

Ludwig Renn, like Arnold Zweig, Anna Seghers, and Bertolt Brecht, is more a product of West Germany than of East Germany. He did not settle permanently in East Germany until 1947. He differs, however, from the first three—and from all other socialist writers—by the fact that he was once a member of the German aristocracy.

Ludwig Renn is a *nom de plume,* which he took from one of

his favorite characters. His real name was Arnold Friedrich Vieth von Goltzenau. He was born in Dresden, the son of a professor who was the tutor of the heir to the throne. He served as an ensign in the royal grenadier regiment, together with the sons of the Saxon king. During the war he was a captain stationed at the western front. After the cessation of hostilities he wrote, on the basis of his regimental log and diary, the documentary novel *Krieg*. Published in 1928, it became an immediate success, like Remarque's *Im Westen nichts Neues*.

Renn is not by nature a writer; in fact, he himself deplores his slowness in arranging his thoughts and his inability to express himself adequately both in speech and in writing. For almost ten years he worked at his manuscript. No publisher would take it. Finally, a good friend shortened it drastically and it appeared in print.

On the blurb of the book, the novel is praised as the record of an unassuming man, an ordinary soldier at the front who merely attempts to describe the war as it was. The style is simple, concise, and colorless; the sentences are short and choppy:

"March!" I commanded. We had to go after them. We climbed over a cattle-fence and came to the brook. There someone was lying in the water, with the red bottom of his trousers showing. On the other side sat, or lay, dead and wounded Frenchmen. I jumped across the brook. Someone back of me scooped up water and lapped it up.

No concession is made to taste or literary charm. The austerity and ingenuousness of the style reflect the character of the author. Although brought up as an aristocrat, he is simple, straightforward, modest, and reserved. By nature he is a soldier—obedient, dutiful, and reliable. He is accustomed to giving and taking commands.

The gracelessness of the style of the narrative by no means militated against the success of *Krieg*. Qute the contrary: it promoted its popularity, for many a reader felt that here was someone who, without literary frills, presented authentic facts and situations.

In part Renn's success was due to the fact that unconsciously he had developed a style that took the public fancy at that time. No longer did the reader seek literary embellishment; he wanted plain facts. Reports, documentary material, and autobiographies came into fashion. It was the era of the new objectivity (*neue Sachlichkeit*). Renn's cool, sober, ascetic prose was entirely in line with the new tendency.

As has been pointed out again and again by critics, the two famous best-sellers about the war, Remarque's and Renn's, have much in common, and, they have often been compared. By sheer coincidence of the spelling of the authors' names, both are frequently listed next to one another in literary reference works. Both books describe personal experiences at the western front during World War I. In both books the former soldiers of all nations that participated between 1914 and 1918 will find their own experiences described.

Fundamentally, however, the two books are different in style, tone, treatment, and aim. Remarque passionately depicts the horror, the inhumanity, and the senselessness of war. He becomes emotional. He appeals to the conscience of the reader; he aims to win him for pacifism. Renn does nothing of the kind. He presents an entirely objective picture; he describes, relates, reports.

In contrast to Renn's lack of literary skill, Remarque was a trained journalist, an editor, and a writer. In *Im Westen nichts Neues* he employs all the possible literary devices to excite, move, amuse, enrage, and dismay the reader. Renn lacked this ability entirely; he shows neither imagination nor emotion, neither sympathy nor sorrow.

The one original device that Renn introduces is his attempt to reproduce the explosive sounds made by the various types of guns, bombs, shells, and shrapnel. Renn's simple, unadorned, and concise sketches are like woodcuts; to some readers they were more convincing than the vivid, colorful scenes of Remarque's broad canvas.

In his next book, *Nachkrieg* (After War), published in 1930, Renn sets out to picture the political and social conditions in Germany of the years 1919 and 1920, again on the basis of personal experiences. Since Renn had become a communist in the meantime, the tone of this work is quite different from that of

Krieg. Instead of an objective report, he presents a propagandist polemic.

The former aristocrat and companion of princes became a deeply devoted and loyal communist. His devotion to communism is highly idealistic, almost religious. In court he had declared that he was a communist because "communist teaching was true"; it was "omnipotent because it was true." Renn had loyally served as an officer in the imperial forces and had obeyed orders without question. With equal loyalty he accepted the commands of his new superiors. The latter expected strong literary support from him. This he was eager to give, but his novels written after 1935 have not lived up to their expectations.

For several years he was the secretary of the League of Proletarian Revolutionary Writers. He put out a communist literary journal, *Linkskurve,* largely at his own expense—he had done very well with the royalties from *Krieg.*

Renn was, however, more interested in military affairs than literature and wrote extensively on military theory, practice, and history. One of his articles in the journal *Aufbruch* got him into trouble with the authorities in 1933. He was arrested, charged with "literary high treason" and condemned to two and a half years' imprisonment. Undoubtedly because of his background and his loyal service, the Nazis became interested in him and tried to win him to their side. Even the personal efforts of Goebbels, Rosenberg, and Hitler failed, however. When he was discharged in 1935, he fled, like many other German writers, to Switzerland.

One trait in Renn's character has never changed: he is a born soldier. He was happy when he could serve again, this time as an officer in the Spanish Civil War, in which he was the commandant of the Thälmann Battalion, Chief of Staff, and head of an officers' school. He describes his experiences in *Der spanische Krieg* (The Spanish War), published in 1955.

After the defeat of the Republican Army in Spain, he went to Mexico where he published *Adel im Untergang* (1944; "downfall of nobility"). In this book Renn recounts his life as an ensign in Dresden, describing in considerable detail his military training, duels, drinking bouts, court balls, parades, receptions, and other social functions. The tone is tender and nostalgic; the social background of the Dresden aristocracy is described with much skill.

In 1947 Renn returned to Europe and settled in East Germany. He was highly esteemed by the party leaders who named him "the classicist of contemporary socialist literature." His loyalty was touching—in fact, unique. Other writers, on occasion, might reveal an inner conflict, disappointment, and dissatisfaction, or express criticism of certain phases of the communist regime, but Renn never. His obedience is unquestioning.

He continued writing, but his works were not always published, for the communist literary arbiters found some of his productions entirely unsuitable. Those that have been printed are often long-winded, boring, and tiresome. His reminiscences, *Meine Kindheit und Jugend* ("my childhood and youth"), which he probably wrote in the Weimar Republic, were not published until 1957. They are of little value. In fact, his novels deteriorated to such a degree, that even the friendly East German critics were embarrassed.

Renn's attempt to record his experiences in the Spanish Civil War is pathetic. Because of the changes in the international scene and in the Communist Party, some of the situations and persons mentioned by Renn in his manuscript had to be deleted. Even after he had made the required deletions, the book was not printed. He had to make further revisions, deletions, and additions. When finally published, the book did contain some interesting and valuable information. As a work of literature, however, it is of no importance. The first edition appeared in 1955 under the title of *Der spanische Krieg*. The revised edition, published in 1959, is entitled *Im spanischen Krieg* ("In the Spanish War").

Of some literary value, and even charm, are the children's books that Renn began writing after 1950. These are all set in exotic lands or in the distant past. Surprisingly enough, Renn here suddenly displays imagination, tenderness, sympathy, and even humor, in sharp contrast to his previous coldly objective style. In the book *Der Neger Nobi* (1955; "The Negro Nobi"), for example, he tells the touching fairytale of the little Negro child who calls upon the animals for help when the slave-traders come into the land.

This change in style and subject matter in Renn's writing is an interesting psychological pehnomenon. Does it represent a longing for more warmth and color? Or is it perhaps a *Flucht nach innen*—a spiritual flight inward?

Hans Marchwitza   (1890–1965)

Hans Marchwitza was outstanding among the so-called *Arbeiterdichter* (worker-writers) whom the East German cultural directors have cultivated with great zeal. In 1964 he was given the National Award, First Class, for Art and Literature. In fact, he received this award three times.

In the official East German directory of writers (*Deutsches Schriftstellerlexikon von den Anfängen bis zur Gegenwart*) Marchwitza is termed "the most important prose writer of the German working class." His works are used as textbooks in the schools. In the basic schoolbook on German literature sixty-six pages are devoted to him. Of his novels it says that they are "of true national significance" and that he continued the tradition of Goethe's *Wilhelm Meister* and Gottfried Keller's *Der grüne Heinrich* "on a higher, socialist level."

Marchwitza was born in 1890, the son of a poor miner in Upper Silesia. In 1910 he went to the Ruhr region, where he worked in the mines. He served in World War I as a noncommissioned officer. Shortly after his discharge he joined the Communist Party.

The desire to write came to him while he worked in the mines. He told how he wrote his first verses on a coal shovel and read them aloud to his fellow workers. In 1924 there was a great strike, at the end of which Marchwitza found himself unemployed. With plenty of time on his hands, he began writing an eyewitness account of what he had experienced. The story of the struggle of the miners for higher wages and better working conditions appeared in 1930 as *Sturm auf Essen* ("storm over the Ruhr"). It was the first of a series of popular books entitled *Der*

Rote 1-Mark Roman ("the red one-mark novel"), which was published by the International Workingmen's Publishing House in Berlin. Within a few weeks *Sturm auf Essen* reached a circulation of 15,000 copies.

Not having had much schooling and no professional training, Marchwitza did not find writing easy. He was quite frank and honest about this, confessing how in the beginning he always had to chew a long time on his pencil before he could compose a sentence. Since the party recognized in him a genuine proletarian author, Marchwitza was given guidance and editorial assistance. He was told to read books. He did so and was particularly attracted by contemporary Soviet authors. Modest and grateful, he says that he was led "by the strong, patient and secure hand of the party," which always gave him "maternal care and recognition." He was even promoted to the editorial board of the monthly literary magazine *Die Linkskurve*.

In 1933 he was forced to flee Germany. From Switzerland and France he went to Spain, where he served in the International Brigade. After having been interned in France, he escaped in 1941 and reached the United States. In New York Marchwitza earned his living as a construction worker and man of odd jobs. In his spare moments he wrote the novel *Meine Jugend* (1947; "my youth"), which Brecht praised highly as "the masterpiece of a poet." In this biographical novel he describes the wretched condition of the Upper Silesian miners during the reign of Kaiser Wilhelm.

In view of his humble origin and authentic proletarian background, the party singled him out as *the* classical writer-worker of contemporary East German literature. He was overwhelmed with honors and awards; his works are published in large editions, and he is constantly praised in East German magazines and newspapers.

His earlier works, however, did not quite fit into communist ideology. Even *Die Kumiaks* (1934; The Kumiaks), which tells the story of a peasant who becomes a miner in the Ruhr and suffers nothing but disappointments, was considered too pessimistic. Since the book appeared abroad as early as 1934, the East German critics thought it unwise to undertake drastic changes.

Marchwitza, however, was prevailed upon to write a second volume, *Die Heimkehr der Kumiaks* (1952; "the return of the Kumiaks"), in which the protagonist, after many bitter experiences, becomes a member of the Communist Party.

In his book *Roheisen* (1955; "crude iron") Marchwitza describes the development of a huge ironworks collective. Although he received the national prize for this book, it was not treated too tenderly by the East German critics.

Despite years of writing and much editorial assistance, it was evident that Marchwitza still had not mastered some elementary rules of grammar and syntax of the German language. Nevertheless, he continued writing and in 1959 published the third volume of the Kumiak trilogy—*Die Kumiaks und ihre Kinder* ("the Kumiaks and their children"). In 1961 he brought out *In Amerika*, in which he gave his impressions of the United States.

The critic Marcel Reich-Ranicki is ruthless in his denunciation of Marchwitza, not as a human being, but as the panegyrically extolled author of East Germany. He asserts baldly that Marchwitza is a simple-minded workman who cannot write. Nevertheless, he has been set up as the highest symbol of literary achievement in East Germany. This would be unthinkable, says Reich-Ranicki, in Poland, Hungary, or Czechoslovakia, and even in Soviet Russia. He doubts whether the East Germans have any literary standards at all.[1]

Others, however, like Anderle, credit him with some ability. Marchwitza's autobiographical novel, *Meine Jugend*, written in New York, presents many colorful scenes, a remarkable naturalness of dialogue, and a firm control of the plot—something he never achieved again. There is little humor in the book, but a fine feeling for descriptive detail.

Erich Weinert   (1890–1953)

Erich Weinert, like many other socialist poets, began his literary career in the early 1920s in the Reich. In 1921 he published his first book of satiric verses, which he recited with great fervor in literary cabarets in Leipzig and Berlin. They were so popular that they were reprinted in socialist papers and magazines.

In 1924 he joined the Communist Party, and his activities as a "singer of the revolution" and political agitator increased. Considered subversive by the authorities, he was arrested and jailed a number of times. With the advent of the Nazis, Weinert fled. For a time he lived in the U.S.S.R., then went to Spain to fight in the Civil War. After being interned in 1939 in France, he returned to the Soviet Union.

There on June 12, 1943, Weinert helped found a national committee of Germans known as Freies Deutschland, of which he was named the president. Other active socialist writers like Willi Bredel, Johannes R. Becher, and Friedrich Wolf joined the committee. While in the Soviet Union he translated the works of a number of Russian poets, which appeared in his *Ausgewählte Gedichte* (1932; "selected poems") and *Rufe in die Nacht* (1947; "cries into the night").

Weinert continued his writing and his political activities after entering East Germany. His earlier satires, written before 1933, were published in 1950 under the title *Das Zwischenspiel, Deutsche Revue von 1918 bis 1933* ("interlude, German review from 1918 to 1933"). East German critics give his verse a high rating because of its wit and satiric flashes, which can be seen in his "Sozialdemokratisches Mailiedchen" (1932; "little social-democratic song"), "Der rote Feuerwehrmann" (1925; "the red fireman"), "An die Armen Europas" (1928; "to the poor of Europe") and "Das Lied von der roten Fahne" (1933; "the song of the red flag"). With unabated enthusiasm Weinert proclaimed the onward sweep of the revolution and its final victory:

> This is the song of the red banner
> That announces the flaming morn;
> Over lands and oceans inspiring,
> To all oppressed hearts it is borne.

Like many of the older East German poets Weinert denounced the war of the "imperialist" powers. A typical stanza from "Der heimliche Aufmarsch" (1927; "the secret line-up") follows:

Workers, listen, they are going to battle,
But not for nation and race.
That is the war of the rulers of the world
Against the working class.
For the war that is now imminent,
That is the war against you, proletarians!

His best poems, according to East German critics, are to be found in his volume *Rufe in die Nacht*. In "Ernst Thälmann" and "Edgar André" he portrays the idealized (socialist) German, in "new, splendid stature."

Weinert was not only a poet but an unusually active and tireless agitator. In the trenches he urged the German soldiers to refuse to continue fighting against the Soviet Union. For propaganda purposes he made effective use of virulent verse that was printed and distributed on leaflets among the troops.

In the poem "An die deutschen Soldaten" (1941; "to the German soldiers") Weinert exhorts them:

A German stretches forth his fraternal hand,
He who believes in his people with all his heart!
Put an end to the pollution of our people!
Whoever is still blind at this turn of the times
Draws Hitler's blood guilt on his own head.

Soldiers, free yourselves from that gang.
Come here, all of you! This is no enemy country.
Come! Save Germany from deepest shame!
Freedom raises its head in the fatherland!
The homeland has recognized the real enemy!
Freedom cries! It lies in your hands!

Weinert's participation in the Spanish Civil War in 1936 resulted in the story "Schlaflose Nacht in Barcelona" (1938; "sleepless night in Barcelona").

The critics proudly proclaimed him the *poeta militans* (fighting poet). He was awarded the National Prize in 1949 and 1952.

Johannes R. Becher (born 1891)

The writer who, according to the East German critics, has made the greatest contribution to their literature, is Johannes R. Becher. Born in 1891 in Munich, he began early as an expressionist poet. Before the end of World War I he became a member of the Communist Party. In view of his ability as a writer he was made an editor of the *Rote Fahne*. Later he organized a group of workmen authors. Because of his tireless political activity, he was shadowed by the police of the Weimar Republic. In 1933 he fled to the Soviet Union.

Discussing Becher's earlier poems, Eduard Engel, in his history of German literature, calls him a *Schreidichter* (screaming poet). He is, however, impressed by Becher's absolute honesty. "One who judges his verse fairly is disarmed by the poet's sincerity; yes, he learns to love him."

Becher himself said that he was "always in revolt" and used this expression as the title of one of his collections of poetry, *Ewig in Aufruhr* (1920; "ever in revolt"). In most of his earlier poems he shouts, shrieks, and lashes about. The basic thought is always freedom. Even though many of his verses are unintelligible to the average person and even nonsensical, the unrestrained vigor and wildness of his language is quite genuine.

Becher himself summarizes his style in the lines:

The poet avoids brilliant harmonies.
He forces through tubas, he beats the drum shrilly,
He incites the people with chopped-off sentences.

Becher makes every effort to create an ear-splitting, nerve-racking atmosphere.

An excellent example of his style is "Hymne an Lenin" ("hymn to Lenin"):

Signs of knocking still in the
Coffins were those of electrically

Executed. Those shot through the belly
Crawled on four feet, plucking into place
Their bowels.—Factory districts; fever-curving
Landscape: clumps of demons, iron-
Square-blocked, swollen, thrown over like
Acidly armored, by illuminating gas
Smoke mantels; by pipe wickerwork
Surrounded, scarred fire-faces;
Waves of force; melting floods of yore. Dream
Thickets wandered through, sawing
Steel beams clamped with tongs, ghostly
Glow-bodies.

An example of his screaming for insurrection:

Come, great flood of the soul, pain, infinite beam!
Destroy the piles, the dam, and the valley!
Burst out of iron throats! Roar, thou voice of steel!
Just let the powers step on thy back,
Evil, too, will prop thee up against countless dross.
Growing, recognize the curses on it!
Bellowing, burn up in water and fire suffering!
Dash, dash, dash against the old, the wretched times!

Becher expresses the typical attitude of the communist poets
toward war; they are all against militarism and plead for peace,
but ardently support the class war and the war against capitalist
systems. Before the outbreak of World War I Becher cried for an
international cataclysm in the words:

O that a conflagration arise like a vault over our heads.
. . . .
We listen for the wild thunderous blasts of the trumpet
And wish for a great world war.

Becher also, occasionally, wrote less frenetic verse. There is,
for example, his poem of six stanzas on Berlin, which begins:

Cement rose, surrounded by cold spots
Lantern domes magically built over:

Around a pipe neck a circus amulet the hedges.
Azure stones burst suddenly out of asphalt basins.
Thou long wept-for bride of the south!
Chopped up dream of childhood. Catholic legend.
At the way of the abyss thou free turning of the morning.

Becher did not, however, merely incite and stir up; he also had visions of a better world.

The new world. . . .
I depict, correctly as far as possible;
A sunny, an extremely organized, a polished landscape
    hovers before me.
An island of happy mankind,
Mankind! Freedom! Love . . . !

After World War I Becher saw in the revolutionary proletariat the fulfillment of his longing for brotherly love and peace on earth. In the "Hymn to Rosa Luxemburg" he celebrates in ecstatic verse that leader of the working class as a saint and a redeemer.

In his poems and short stories Becher had always tiraded against imperialism and had presented a vision of a better world. His expressionistic style did not, however, fit into the literary program of the party functionaries, who felt that he was not reaching the proletarian masses. Closer cooperation with the socialist press, an intensive reading of the works of Gorki, and a study of Lenin's statements on the role and aim of party literature, brought about a change in his style after 1926. His verse became clearer and simpler, so that it was intelligible to the ordinary worker. Examples of this are his poems "Tod des Arbeitslosen" ("death of the unemployed"), "Städte" ("cities"), and "Stein" ("stone"), in which he stressed the plight of the exploited worker (1928).

The ecstatic and rhapsodic phases of the poems of his expressionist period were replaced by greater clarity and simplicity. From an intellectual anarchist he turned into a disciplined communist. One of the basic themes of his verse now was *Anderswerden*—becoming different, i.e., the development of the new, socialist individual in society and his portrayal in literature. His trans-

formation was so complete that he was named the official poet of
the state (1953) and made Minister of Culture (1954).

Formerly Becher had expressed pacifistic attitudes in opposi-
tion to war; now he became aggressive. He lashed out against the
preparation for a renewed imperialist war in the novel *Levisite*
(1926), but at the end presented a vision of the only just war—
the war of the proletariat.

Becher was also very active as a propagandist and organizer,
constantly urging the worker to revolutionary action. He celebrates this type of proletarian in a volume of poems *Ein Mensch
unserer Zeit* (1929; "a man of our time"). In an ambitious choral
work, *Der große Plan* (1931; "the great plan"), he rhapsodizes
over the new era of mankind. This thought was one of the basic
contributions of Becher to the development of the concept of
socialist realism. The new man was to be a champion and a crea-
tor of a "beautiful human community" (*eine schöne Menschenge-
meinschaft*).

Becher had been profoundly shocked by the triumph of National Socialism in Germany. A sensitive soul, he felt a personal
responsibility for the debasement of the German people and the
injustice that prevailed. He expresses this in "Tränen des Vater-
landes Anno 1937" ("tears of the fatherland in the year 1937").
He was deeply ashamed of the crimes committed by the Nazis all
over Europe and sought relief by expressing in verse his nostalgic
feelings for the landscape of his childhood.

Becher was a member of the so-called Freies Deutschland, a
committee formed by German exiles which met in Moscow in
July 1943 and planned to hasten the defeat of the Nazis and
establish a socialist Germany. In consonance with these aims,
Becher wrote a dramatic poem "Schlacht um Moskau" (1942;
"battle for Moscow"). It tells of a young soldier in the Wehr-
macht who begins to think about the war and finally refuses to
serve the barbaric system any longer.

While living in Russia Becher developed an even simpler
style of expression. This is shown especially in "Das Holzhaus"
(1938; "the wooden house"). Becher always expresses the warm-
est affection for his homeland and the bitterest hatred toward
those who were besmirching the name of Germany. A good ex-

ample of this is the poem "Schöne deutsche Heimat" ("beautiful German homeland"), which contains the lines:

> Oh how beautiful the mountain scene glows
> In its glacier brilliance,
> And the Alpine meadows nestle
> Against the fields of rubble,
> Dark green,
> The edelweiss enticed.
> But midst all this beauty
> There lay
> Surrounded by an electric barbed-wire fence
> The concentration camp. . . .
> Therefore home is truly beautiful only there
> Where man has created human order for himself,
> Human beauty.

Some of his ballads are even simpler and clearer, as for example the brief one entitled "Ballade von den Dreien" ("ballad of the three").

> The officer said: "Bury the Jew."
> The Russian retorted: "No!"
>
> So they placed him in the grave.
> The Jew defiantly said: "No!"
>
> The officer cried: "Bury them both!"
> A German stepped out and said, "No!"
>
> The officer said: "Put him beside the two!
> Bury him too! And *he* calls himself a German!"
>
> And Germans also buried the German. . . .

Realizing that the strength of the newly established East German republic depended on the younger generation, Becher appeals directly to youth in many of his later poems. He dedicated his *Neue deutsche Volkslieder* (1951; "new German folksongs") to the younger generation. Hanns Eisler composed the music for these songs that express their joy over the beauty of the German landscape. Becher's aim was to build up a new *Heimats-*

bewußtsein, i.e., a feeling for one's native region. Here and there the dark spots of the past show themselves, but these are dispelled by the light flooding the landscape. In *Deutsche Sonette* (1952; "German sonnets") the political aspect is stressed; the poet expresses his deep longing for a united Germany.

In his collection of verse entitled *Schritt der Jahrhundertmitte* (1958; "midcentury step") Becher strikes a semi-religious tone. He speaks of the tragedy that results from the disproportion between the infinite possibilities of mankind and the limitations of the individual. The "great deed" is the transformation of man in the socialist community. Death is overcome by the superior power of the great and infinite in man's achievements.

> The whole man, as he is
> in thought, feeling, and will,
> With all that separated, that bound him
> In all his depths, his stillness. . . .
>
> The whole man we want to seize,
> Loving and hating him, and comprehend
> The whole enormous human being.

In this poem Becher expresses the esthetic program and ideal that determined socialist literature in its years of struggle against Nazism. This encompassing of the entire human being was supposed to lead to a free and democratic Germany.

Becher himself said: "The problems of poetry do not lie where it is generally assumed, certainly not in technical skill, but in life, in the view of life, in the depths of the development of personality. An act does not begin with new types of forms, it begins always with a new human being."

One of the best examples of Becher's simpler style and of the fact that he can express his basic ideas clearly is the East German national anthem, which he composed. The last of the three stanzas follows:

> Let us plow, let us build,
> Learn, and toil as never before,
> And relying on its strength,

A free people comes to the fore.
German youth, the noblest striving
Of our people joined in you.
If you become Germany's new life
The sun will shine more beautifully
Than ever over Germany.

Bertolt Brecht *(1898–1956)*

The outstanding socialist writer, and the only one who has enjoyed world fame, is Bertolt Brecht. Although he is claimed by
the East Germans, his reputation as a dramatist rests on four or
five plays written in West Germany and on his five greatest
dramas all written in exile. His popular *Die Dreigroschenoper*
(1928; The Threepenny Opera), an entertaining but hardly
serious musical, was composed during the years of the Weimar
Republic.

Bertolt Brecht was born February 10, 1898, in Augsburg, Bavaria, the son of the manager of a paper mill. His father was
Catholic; his mother, who came from the Black Forest, Protestant.
Brecht was closely attached to her but felt instinctively drawn to
the city rather than to the country. He introduces himself in two
stanzas of the poem entitled "Vom armen B.B." (1921; "about
poor B.B.") as follows:

I, Bertolt Brecht, am from the black forests.
My mother carried me into the cities.

He continues by saying that the coldness of the forest will
ever remain with him; that he feels himself at home in the asphalt city where he has newspapers, tobacco, and brandy. In a
final line he characterizes himself as suspicious and lazy, but con-
tented.

Actually Brecht was never lazy; in fact, he was a prolific
writer, beginning at the age of sixteen. But he was cautious and
crafty. Even as a child he was sensitive and rebellious in a quiet,
negative way. He was contemptuous of respectability in any form
and always yearned for the company of plebians. On both his

father's and his mother's side his ancestors had been shrewd, hardheaded peasants. His basic character traits may have had their foundation there. Throughout his life he always approached intellectual as well as practical matters in a calculated and cunning manner.[1]

Brecht was sixteen when World War I broke out. He soon got into trouble at the Realgymnasium he attended by expressing sharply worded pacifist views. Even at this early age he was already contributing book reviews and poems to a local paper.

In 1916 he left school and moved to Munich where he studied medicine at the university. Soon he was drafted; being a medical student, he was made a medical orderly in a military hospital. His gruesome activities there left lasting traces in his character. His poetry is haunted by images of dismembered bodies; a fanatical anti-militarism became the basis of all his political thought. His essentially tender mind was shaken to the core by the sheer horror of existence in a world where such suffering was allowed to prevail.

As a student Brecht drifted into the milieu of smoke-filled cafés and taverns. There he would sing his ballads, accompanying himself on the guitar or banjo and bawling out the words in his high-pitched voice. Sometimes he was beaten up by soldiers who took exception to his slurs on the army.

One of Brecht's most famous ballads and also one of his earliest is "Legende vom toten Soldaten" (Legend of the Dead Soldier), a poem of nineteen stanzas that he wrote in 1918. It treats the macabre theme of a dead soldier being disinterred and sent back to war.

Since the war had dragged on into the fifth spring, the soldier decided to die a hero's death.

> Because the war was not quite done
> It made the Kaiser blue
> To think the soldier lay there dead
> Before his time came due.

The soldier slept on during the summer, then the grave was inspected. The medical mission trailed out to the little cemetery and disinterred what was left of the fallen soldier. The doctor looked the corpse over carefully and found the soldier fit for duty —the shirking coward!

So they took the soldier with them and tried to rouse him with fiery schnapps. Two nurses and his wife clung to his arms. And because he stank of rot a priest limped on before, waving an incense burner so that the putrid odor would not be too apparent. The music played a lively march and the soldier strutted along as he had been taught. Two hospital orderlies supported him so that he did not fall into the mud.

A man in formal attire strode on ahead with proudly bulging chest, for, as a German citizen, he knew exactly what to do. The soldier marched on, down the high road, through villages, where dogs barked at him and women waved to him. There was much hurrahing and drumming. The soldier bravely dies the death of a hero, as told in the closing lines:

> But the soldier, as he had been taught,
> Goes to his hero's death.

Brecht achieves a highly ironic effect by sometimes introducing into an earthy ballad a few lines from some well-known classic as a refrain. In the "Liturgie vom Hauch" ("liturgy on breath") he quotes after every stanza, with a few slight changes, the first six lines of Goethe's famous poem "Wanderers Nachtlied." The full effect of this is apparent only when one appreciates the fact that this stanza is regarded with almost religious reverence by most Germans. It has been said that Goethe's eight-line poem is made up of the twenty-four most beautiful words in German verse.

Brecht's ballad begins with the description of an old woman who dies of hunger on the street. A doctor, a socially-minded citizen, and a commissar appear in succession. Finally, a group of workers come along who are shot down by the military.

> Then suddenly there came many red men
> Who wanted to talk with the military
> But the military talked with machinegun fire,
> And then the red men said nothing more.
> But they still had a wrinkle on their foreheads.

> Then the birds in the woods were silent,
> O'er all the tree-tops there is calm.
> From all the peaks you feel the balm
> Of barely a breath of air.

The poem ends abruptly with a drastic denouement. Suddenly a big red bear appears who knows nothing of the local customs, for he comes from beyond the sea. He eats up all the little birds in the woods.

> The little birds no longer were silent,
> O'er all the tree-tops there is unrest.
> And from the peaks you now feel the zest
> Of a breath of air.

Brecht employs the same device in "Großer Dankchoral" (Grand Choral of Thanksgiving), in which he takes a majestic hymn known to all Germans ("Lobet den Herrn") and paraphrases it with bitter ironic gibes. The closing lines are:

> Praise with your hearts the unmindfulness of heaven!
> Since it knows not
> Either your name or your face
> No one knows that you are still there.

> Praise the cold, the darkness and corruption!
> Look upward:
> There's no concern about you
> And you can die without worry.

It is significant that Brecht began by writing and reciting verse at an early age. Throughout his life he remained essentially a poet; it was his primary mode of expression. His plays are filled with poetry.

His earliest collection of verse, published in 1927, bears the ironic title *Hauspostille* (Manual of Piety). The poems of this volume are a revolt against contemporary social conditions and especially against war. Although he expresses a hope for the future, he often manifests a deep skepticism. Brecht's poetry is basically a reaction against the individualism of western European poets; he was a social-minded, political poet.[2]

Many of his poems deal with the problem of human suffering. A convinced materialist, he avoided romantic emotions and sought the ultimate meaning of life in a rational, political organization of mankind. As an ardent Marxist he sought to spread socialist theory; a definite didactic strain runs through many of his poems. Rejecting emotion and romanticism, he found esthetic values in the purely functional. Because of this, he was often extremely economical in his use of words. He was, however, fundamentally philosophic and severely moral.

Brecht was especially successful with the folk ballad, in which he combined older, traditional forms of imagery with modern, realistic satire. This is evident in such selections as "Ballade von des Cortez Leuten" (Ballad of Cortez Men), "Die Ballade von dem Soldaten" (The Ballad of the Soldier), "Das Lied von der Eisenbahn-Truppe von Fort Donald" (The Song of the Railroad Gang of Fort Donald), and "Ballade von den Aberteuern" (Ballad of the Adventurers).

A great part of the success of Brecht's ballads was due to the fact that he composed them to the accompaniment of a guitar. Singable, they became immensely popular among workers everywhere.

Another type of verse that Brecht developed successfully is the short, unrhymed poem, which appears in many of his plays and which he called a *Gestich*. These short pieces are suggestive of Chinese poetry. The tone is often Biblical, for despite Brecht's irreligious attitude, he had a high regard for the Scriptures. Some of his short poems are so brief that they are practically aphorisms in verse.

> On the Wall There was Written in Chalk:
>> They want war.
>> He who wrote it
>> Has already fallen.

> When the Leaders Speak of Peace,
>> Do the common people know
>> That war is coming?

When the leaders curse war,
The enlistment orders have
    already been issued.

1939: Few News Items Come from the Reich.
    The house painter speaks of great times to come.
    The woods still grow.
    The fields still bear.
    The cities still stand.
    Men still breathe.

One of Brecht's basic thoughts was that this world is so evil that it is impossible to be entirely good. This is the thesis that he develops in the play *Der gute Mensch von Sezuan* (1943; The Good Woman of Setzuan). He also expresses it in a number of his poems, as in the "Elegie," which begins:

These are, indeed, dark times in which I live!
To say a guileless thing is foolish;
A smooth brow bespeaks insensitivity.
To laugh is to be someone who
Has not yet received the
Frightful news.

Brecht continues, in the first person, to deplore the unhappiness of the times. Even simple conversation is almost a crime because it includes silence concerning atrocities. A man calmly crossing the street may be in desperate need, beyond the reach of friends. Physically the poet has been well taken care of, but he has been spared purely by chance. If his luck runs out, he is lost.

He is told to eat, drink, and be merry, but how can he eat and drink if he takes it from someone who is hungry and when someone who is thirsty has to go without a glass of water? Would that he were wise and possessed the wisdom of the old books, able to keep out of the world's strife, and survive without resort to violence, returning good for evil.

.All of which I cannot do,
These are, indeed, dark times in which I live.

At times Brecht's expressions of despair over the failures of mankind and sorrow over the unattainability of the ideal become grotesque, almost clownish. This is strikingly so in *"Das Lied von der Unzulänglichkeit menschlichen Strebens"* (The Song of the Inadequacy of Man's Striving), from the *Die Dreigroschenoper*.

> For this world we live in
> None of us is smart enough.
> Never do we notice
> All is lie and bluff.

Man is not good at all,
Hit him on the hood.
And if you have hit him
Perhaps he'll then be good.

> Yes, for this life, poor fellow,
> Man isn't very good.
> So just continue hitting
> Him soundly on the hood.

The austerity of Brecht's verse is especially evident in the poems of his later period. These were collected in *Lieder, Gedichte, und Chöre* (1934) and *Svendborger Gedichte* (1937). Many of the poems are extremely functional, with sharp and incisive statements. Sometimes Brecht mingles his irony with a bit of emotional pathos. He is particularly bitter in "Keiner oder Alle" ("none or all").

The poem begins:

Slave, who will free you?
Those who stand in the deepest depths
Will, comrade, see you,
And they will hear your crying.
Slaves will free you.

> None or all. All or nothing.
> One alone cannot save himself.
> Guns or chains.
> None or all. All or nothing.

The poem concludes:

Who, lost one, will dare it?
He who no longer can bear his misery
Must join those who out of necessity
Have already seen to it that the word is
Today and not tomorrow.

Brecht's mood, however, is not always somber: he has written many cheerful popular songs and charming children's poems. One of the most delightful is "Der Pflaumenbaum" ("the plum tree").

In the yard stands a plum tree;
It's little, one would hardly believe it.
There's a fence around it,
So that no one will step on it.

Two stanzas follow. The little tree would like to get bigger but it has too little sun. One can hardly believe that it is a plum tree because it never bears a plum. But it is a plum tree—you can tell by the leaf.

As an example of how the East German literary critic evaluates a simple little poem like this, the following passage is quoted from *Deutsche Literaturgeschichte*. It appears directly before the three stanzas of "Der Pflaumenbaum."

In the ballads, the songs, and the children's songs, Brecht attained an extraordinary concentration and popular appeal. Here the tradition of the classic German ballad is evident. Above all, undertones of Gottfried August Bürger can be heard. The popularity of the poems rests on their socialistic slant. Even in the simplest verses Brecht's conscious attitude in favor of the class struggle of the workers is evident. He always makes it clear that the existing capitalist system must be changed.[3]

Almost from the very start of his career Brecht assumed certain external characteristics that he retained for life. He was always unshaven and allowed his hair to fall over his forehead in an untidy manner. His garments were unpressed and sloppy; he wore steel-rimmed glasses and smoked the cheapest cigars.

When the Russian Revolution came in November of 1918,

Brecht was wholeheartedly on the side of the revolutionaries. Evidently this did not appeal to him, for he was soon again an easygoing medical student in Munich. He became interested in the theater and began to write plays. Having read one by Hanns Johst, *Der Einsame* ("the lonely one"), he wagered a friend that he could write a better play in four days on the same theme. The play he produced, *Baal* (1922), depicts a completely anti-social poet. Brecht realized that this wild and extravagant piece had little chance of being performed, so he wrote another play, entitled *Spartakus*. Lion Feuchtwanger, the novelist and playwright, helped him with it. It was renamed *Trommeln in der Nacht* (1922; Drums in the Night) and became Brecht's first stage success. It was performed in Munich on September 29, 1922.

The performance in Munich was a great success. Right from the start Brecht introduced some of his basic notions of stagecraft. To produce the alienation of his audience from the characters, which he considered very important, he had the walls of the theater adorned with signs reading: "Don't stare so romantically" and "Every man feels best in his own skin." His insistence on supervising every last detail and making continual changes involved him in endless quarrels with actors and stage managers, as well as decorators and artists. At times it caused so much dissension that the production of a play had to be given up. This happened in Berlin, where *Trommeln in der Nacht* was a failure.

Brecht, however, was not dictatorial by nature. He was always the center of a crowd of collaborators, asking advice and readily accepting it. Puffing his cheap cigar he would stalk through the room listening to arguments, pro and con. He was so ready to make changes, that there were sometimes two dozen versions of one play.[4]

After the beercellar putsch in Munich, Brecht went to Berlin, whose literary and theatrical world he loved. His play *Im Dickicht der Städte* (1923; In the Jungle of Cities) was to be performed at the Deutsches Theater and *Edward II* was to follow. He was very industrious, writing poems, short stories, articles, and plays. *Mann ist Mann* (1927; Man is Man) was his first comedy. Two great figures of the German stage, Piscator and Reinhardt, appreciating his talent, collaborated with him.

Meanwhile Brecht read Marx's *Das Kapital,* which influenced his political thinking considerably. Far more important for him, however, from the artistic point of view, was his collaboration with the composer Kurt Weill. Brecht had always sung his own ballads to the guitar, composing the music with the words. Later he also made up his own music for any songs or ballads that occurred in his plays. In this he was helped by his faithful secretary Elisabeth Hauptmann.

Brecht's attitude toward music was highly idiosyncratic. He hated Beethoven and the sound of violins but liked Bach and Mozart. Above all he disliked the dignified atmosphere of the concert hall. Weill shared Brecht's contempt for neoromantic music; he sought a return to a popular, modern form of musical expression.

At the music festival in Baden-Baden he performed his operatic cantata *Mahagonny,* which formed the germ of the full-length opera *Aufstieg und Fall der Stadt Mahagonny* (1929; Rise and Fall of the City of Mahagonny). This and *Die Dreigroschenoper* were the greatest successes of the cooperation between Weill and Brecht. They made them both famous. In connection with the opera as with so many plays of Brecht, there were outbursts of indignation and scandals. The biggest row was concerned with the film version. The film, however, after many delays and a court case, was finished and was immensely successful.

Fascinated with Marxist philosophy, Brecht decided to work it into a play. He wrote *Die Maßnahme* (The Measures Taken), which the communist literary authorities frowned upon. Nevertheless he determined to continue to cooperate with them. He made an adaptation of Gorki's *Mat';* the result was *Die Mutter* (1932; The Mother), a moving and impressive play, despite its propagandist tendencies.

Deeply moved by the wretched winter of 1930–31 in Berlin, when unemployment was at its highest, Brecht set out to write a play showing how capitalist society functions. The result was *Die heilige Johanna der Schlachthöfe* (1932; St. Joan of the Stockyards), one of his greatest and most characteristic works.

Brecht's bizarre appearance annoyed many respectable people, which was precisely what he intended. He loved being taken for a dangerous fellow. He attempted to destroy the traditional image of the poet as romantic, withdrawn, and delicate. He deliberately assumed an unromantic and businesslike air. In the circle of his own admirers, however, he lost the sinister air he liked to wear in public. He became kind and gentle; he had a genius for friendship.

His first marriage to Marianne Zoff ended in divorce. He then married the gifted actress Helene Weigel, who played the leading role in many of his plays. She combined the emotional intensity of a great actress with an acute and cultivated mind. Her loyalty and devotion to Brecht never faltered.

On February 27, 1933, fire broke out in the Reichstag building and storm troopers began rounding up communists and left-wing intellectuals. On the following day Brecht went into exile. He fled to Vienna with his wife and little son Stefan. Brecht was number five on the list of those to be arrested by the Nazis. He was deprived of his German citizenship, and his books were among the first to be thrown into the flames.

Brecht sought a place to live and work. Finally, at the invitation of a Danish novelist, he went to Denmark. He repeatedly visited Paris and London to discuss the possibility of having one of his plays performed. Finally, toward the end of 1935, the left-wing Theater Union in New York decided to put on *Die Mutter*. Brecht came over and tried to prevent the company from changing his style to a conventional one. The performance was not a success.

In 1936 Brecht became co-editor of the antifascist literary review *Das Wort*, published in Moscow. It is significant that during his exile he rarely visited Moscow and then only for a few days.

Brecht wrote a series of poems and satires as anti-Nazi propaganda. They were published in one volume, *Svendborger Gedichte*. The most virulent verse against the war is contained in the first part, entitled "Deutsche Kriegsfibel" ("German war primer"). Strangely enough, his communist point of view hindered him from penetrating the true nature of National Socialism and he missed entirely its more sinister aspects.

Political oversimplification is the weakness of his only large-scale novel, *Der Dreigoschenroman* (Threepenny Novel), published in Amsterdam in 1934. Obviously he was more skilled in and more deeply interested in the literary and poetical phases of writing. From 1937 on he threw off the shackles of political propaganda and began to write a series of plays that showed his talent undiminished. While in Denmark he wrote a number of his outstanding plays: *Leben des Galilei* (1943, 1947, 1954; Galileo), *Das Verhör des Lukullus* (1940; The Trial of Lucullus), *Der gute Mensch von Sezuan*, and *Mutter Courage und ihre Kinder* (1941; Mother Courage and Her Children). He also took part in a left-wing theater in Copenhagen.

In the summer of 1939, when war had become inevitable, he moved to Sweden. Next he went to Finland. In preparation for his removal to America he wrote a play for the U.S. stage: *Der aufhaltsame Aufstieg des Arturo Ui* (The Resistible Rise of Arturo Ui), a transposition of the rise of Hitler into a Chicago gangster atmosphere. At the beginning of June 1941 Brecht, his family, and some members of his circle set out on the long journey to America by Siberian Express to Vladivostok. It was a last-minute escape.

Since he could find no publisher to print his poems, he circulated them in mimeographed form. He continued writing plays, however, producing the remarkable *Der kaukasische Kreidekreis* (1945; The Caucasian Chalk Circle). Living in Santa Monica, he continued to go unshaven and tieless, and to smoke five-cent cigars. He stood out as the main figure of the German-speaking colony.

Ironically enough, Brecht, whose early writing had centered around a mythical conception of a startling American world, had no understanding for America. He had no contact with its culture, distrusted its politics, and disliked its food. He did not even admire the magnificent forests of California.

Slowly he gained a foothold in the United States. Shortly after settling in California, he met Eric Bentley, who became his chief advocate. The conquest of the American stage was not easy. His *Furcht und Elend des Dritten Reiches* (Private Life of the Master Race) was shown in New York in 1945 and got a very unfavorable reception. His production of *Leben des Galilei* in

Beverly Hills was also a failure. Charles Laughton was magnificent in his role, but he did not win over the audience.

In September of 1947 Brecht received a subpoena to appear before the Committee on Un-American Activities and to testify. With tongue in cheek Brecht handled the situation with such cleverness and cunning that he completely confused the members of the committee, who had not read his plays. At the close of the session the chairman thanked him profusely for his exemplary behavior as a most cooperative witness. Brecht left Washington, having decided to return to Europe. He went first to Switzerland, where a number of his plays were performed in Zurich.

In October of 1948 Brecht arrived in East Berlin. He was given a warm official reception. His play, *Mutter Courage und ihre Kinder,* in which his wife acted, was a brilliant success. It was the beginning of the Berlin Ensemble.

Upon his return to Zurich, Brecht had an important decision to make. The communists of East Germany were very eager to have him. He was attracted by their generous offers, but he was cautious. Although a communist, he did not want to move too far into the Soviet orbit. He knew the hardships and restrictions of East Germany; he appreciated the freedom and the comforts of the West. With peasant cunning he put the copyright of his works in the hands of a West German publisher, applied for Austrian citizenship, put his money in Swiss banks, and later bought himself a house in Denmark! Thus he was financially secure, could travel freely, and was beyond the restrictions that communist literary arbiters might try to impose. In fact, there is some doubt that Brecht was ever a card-carrying communist.

In the fall of 1949 he moved to East Berlin to become the artistic adviser to the Berlin Ensemble. He still wore a workman's suit, a cloth cap, the metal-rimmed glasses, and drove an old Steyr cabriolet. He was perfectly happy contributing to the development of the Schiffbauerdamm Theater.

Despite Brecht's successes and honors, his relations with the East German authorities were not smooth. He had become a communist in protest against the empty nationalism of the German bourgeoisie and now found himself supporting a regime which indulged in a propaganda that was even more chauvinistic and hollow. There was continual wrangling about his plays. Nevertheless, Brecht remained loyal to the communists. He courageously defended his ideas, however, despite his being let down repeatedly. Once the leading monthly *Der Monat* appeared with a blank page, where Brecht's article on artistic freedom was to have appeared.

The struggles with the communists took a great deal out of him. After a while he began to look tired and worn. After his return to East Berlin he failed to produce anything of major importance. The authorities were continually urging him to write plays expounding the communist ideology. Brecht tried to please them by adapting a number of earlier pieces by other writers but never quite succeeded.

He traveled much, visiting Paris, which he loved. In the spring of 1955 he fell seriously ill. On his fifty-eighth birthday, February 10, 1956, Brecht was in Milan to attend a production of *The Threepenny Opera*. He had a foreboding of his approaching end, saying to a friend, "At least one knows that death will be easy. A slight knock at the windowpane, and then. . . ."

He continued his work in East Berlin but his condition deteriorated. On August 14, 1956, he died of a coronary thrombosis. He was buried, at his request, in the old Huguenot cemetery beneath the window of his last apartment. He had forbidden any speechmaking at the funeral. In his apartment an enormous mass of manuscripts, draft plays, diaries, and jottings of all sorts was found.

The theater of Brecht was something new in theory and practice. Rejecting the Aristotelian drama, he developed the so-called epic theater, in which the principle of alienation (*Verfremdungseffekt*) was a basic element. According to this, the audience should not be made to feel any emotion; it should be made to think. Identification with the characters of the play makes thinking impossible. Therefore, the theater must do its best to destroy in the bud any illusion of reality. The epic theater is historical; the audience gets a report of past events. The spectators must be kept separate, estranged, alienated from the action. The theater is a stage and not the world itself.[5]

In the beginning Brecht's theater was strictly didactic. Later he admitted the idea of entertainment, but only the pleasure that the scientist feels on discovering a new mystery of the universe. In the epic theater there is no attempt to fix highly individualized character. Character emerges from the social function of the individual and changes with that function.

The actor does not impersonate a character; he merely narrates the actions; he goes through the motions, he quotes. The epic theater seeks to prevent the identification of the audience with the characters, and the identification of the actor with the character. The epic theater is extrovert; the inner life is irrelevant. Characters acting and reacting upon each other are the basic unit of the Brecht theater. The songs, decor, lighting, and musical numbers are interrupting features, introduced to help create alienation.

Although Brecht's productions are now a part of world literature, only one play, *Die Dreigroschenoper*, ever achieved real popular success, and that only in the English version, translated by Eric Bentley. It is a free adaptation of John Gay's *Beggar's Opera*. Polly, the daughter of Peachum, king of the beggars, marries Macheath, a thief. Peachum disapproves and wants his son-in-law hanged. Macheath is warned but remains in London. He is arrested and condemned. As he stands on the scaffold a messenger arrives with the queen's pardon, the award of a country house, and a pension of 10,000 pounds. The play ends with a solemn chorus, imploring mankind to forgive all malefactors.

One of Brecht's fundamental notions was the helplessness of man, his inability to influence the world around him, as in the *Legende des toten Soldaten*. In *Baal* one of the striking images is that of a man drifting downstream, carried along helplessly by the current.

Brecht's entire literary work is concerned with the problem of the struggle between subconscious impulse and conscious control. He made increasingly strenuous efforts at calculated, active self-control and tried to become wholly rational and impersonal. Ostentatiously he rejected all sentiment and emotion. But his sensitive nature required a stronger and more positive discipline than he could provide for himself. This he found in communism. It rejected the existing world with its cruelty and absurdities; it provided a technique of self-control, rational thought, and discipline. It claimed to be entirely scientific.[6]

Despite his pacifism, or rather anti-militarism, Brecht believed in the use of force. If man can be transformed by violent methods into something evil, he can also be made into something better by the practices of the communist social engineers. Communism, or rather his own brand of it, provided the focus around which he could integrate the forces that pulled his split personality in many directions.

In his plays he pictures the predicament of man and the irony of human conditions as seen by James Joyce, Kafka, and the French existentialists. The world is evil; virtue brings no reward. Human nature is pretty much the same; the poor are mean and the rich are ruthless and cruel. War is the natural state of man. There is no justice. In *Der kaukasische Kreidekreis* (1948; the Caucasian Chalk Circle) the only innocent person who wins in the end is the servant girl Grusche. Life continues only because mothers doggedly and irrationally persist in rearing their young. It is a world sullied by evil. The place of fate is taken by the inscrutable workings of the social order, which molds the lives of characters. But this is only half the picture. On the positive side there is the hope of communism.

Curiously enough, however, Brecht in his plays presents the negative side with greater skill, conviction, and color. One is reminded of Milton's *Paradise Lost,* Goethe's *Faust*, and Dante's *Inferno*. The new, unfolding world is merely postulated, assumed, taken for granted.

During his eight years in East Germany Brecht was unable to produce a single convincing play on the realities of life in the communist world, even though it lay immediately before him. The authorities begged him to picture socialist well-being; he was simply unable to do it. Brecht's plays fail to convey the message that man has been redeemed by a radical change in the social order. His characters, particularly his women—Joan Dark, Simone Marchard, Mother Courage, Shen Te, and Grusche— redeem themselves by their courage in the face of overwhelming adversities.

His estranging devices, too, were startling but not successful.

He succeeded in reducing the emotional identification of audience and characters, but never evoked the rational, critical attitude. In fact, his leading characters, especially the women, are so profoundly human, that the audience is always deeply moved with pity. The plethora of parody, caricature, irony, and denunciation in the plays does not arouse indignation at the social order; the audience is not led to a support of Marxism. Toward the end Brecht himself seemed to realize that he had failed in his struggle to secure an acceptance of his theories. In his last theoretical essays he even suggested the expression "dialectical theater" in place of "epic theater."

Brecht believed that his epic theater was the truly Marxist theater, but the communists did not agree. The Brechtian theater exists only on the fringes of the communist world. The doctrines of Stanislavsky, the theater of identification and illusion, remain the prescribed, official norm for actors and directors from Vladivostok to Moscow.

Brecht's basic ideas are reflected in his first stage success, *Trommeln in der Nacht.* This comedy in five acts takes place in the Berlin of 1919. Kragler, a soldier returning from the war after years of captivity in Africa, finds his fiancée engaged to a black-market profiteer. During the engagement party Kragler appears like a ghost from the past and demands his fiancée. Anna, pregnant, still loves him. As he wanders through the streets he is pursued by her. He is about to join the Spartakists—a group of dissident socialists—in their uprising of January, 1919, when Anna appears and asks forgiveness. Kragler rejects the revolutionaries with the words: "My flesh is to rot in the gutter so that your ideals may reach heaven. Are you drunk!" He prefers the comfortable role of a married man to that of a hero, remarking, "I am a swine and the swine goes home."

Trommeln in der Nacht is one of the best plays about returning soldiers. For the production scheduled by the Berlin Ensemble, the communist literary dictators asked Brecht to offset the anti-revolutionary cynicism of Kragler. So he introduced some references to an ardent youth who dies a hero's death. This interlude is hardly noticed; the play remains a firm rejection of all heroic cant, whether military or revolutionary. Kragler is in the grip of an emotion beyond his conscious control. He chooses what instinct dictates; that is, he decides in favor of a peaceful life of passive mediocrity. He refuses to help change society. His choice is a victory of instinct over rational, premeditated action.

The problem of the struggle between subconscious impulse and conscious control and the problem of the helplessness of man are brought out forcefully in the comedy *Mann ist Mann*, based on Kipling's *Barrack-Room Ballads*. Galy Gay, an Irish dockworker, a mild little man who cannot say no, goes out to buy a fish for his wife for supper. He meets three British soldiers who have tried to rob a pagoda and have lost their fourth man, Jeriah Jip, in the turmoil. Since they would be identified as the thieves if they failed to produce the fourth man at roll call, they decide that Galy Gay must be transformed into the soldier Jeriah Jip. One man, they argue, is as good as another. The verse at the end of each act stresses the idea in the refrain, "A man's a man."

The soldiers persuade Galy to try to sell a fake elephant, made of a stuffed head and cardboard. He is seized as a lawbreaker and sentenced to be shot. He is put through a mock execution. When he awakens, his mind is blank. He consents to pronounce the funeral oration for Galy Gay. Persuaded that he is the soldier Jeriah Jip, he takes part in the campaign in Tibet and captures a fortress singlehanded.

This play marks the turning point from Brecht's youthful anarchic nihilism to the awareness of the power of society. Quite drastically he shows how malleable man is. With amazing intuition Brecht grasped the essence of later brainwashing techniques. Three brutal soldiers wipe out Galy Gay's individuality; he becomes a fighting machine, molded like a piece of clay.

The struggle between reason and instinct, between subconscious impulse and rational control is magnificently portrayed in the historic *Leben des Galilei*. There are three versions of this play; the final one has fifteen scenes. It is the year 1609; Galileo, now forty-five years old, lives with his daughter Virginia, his housekeeper Mrs. Sarti, and her little son, Andrea, a promising pupil. He earns a meager living as a lecturer at the University of Padua. Quite unscrupulous, he does not hesitate to claim that he invented the telescope after merely copying it from a Dutch invention.

Accepting an invitation of the Duke of Florence, he leaves Venice. The Inquisition forbids him to publish his scientific findings that support the Copernican theory that the earth revolved around the sun. For eight years he remains silent, until a new Pope, Urban VIII, who is an enlightened mathematician, ascends the throne. Galileo appeals to him, but the Grand Inquisitor persuades the Pope that the church's authority would be undermined. As a warning the Pope agrees that Galileo be shown the instruments of torture used by the Inquisition.

His faithful pupils, among them Andrea Sarti, refuse to believe that the great scientist will recant. The tolling of the bells announces that he has recanted. When he enters, a broken man, Andrea cries out, "Pity the country that has no heroes!" Galileo replies, "No, pity the country that needs heroes!"

For years Galileo is compelled to live in the country under the close surveillance of the Inquisition. Nearly blind, he is apparently dominated by his daughter, whose fiancé left her because of Galileo's views. Andrea Sarti is disgusted at the old man's cowardice, but his contempt turns into admiration when Galileo hands him the completed manuscript of his *Discorsi*, written in secret. Nevertheless, Galileo regards himself as a criminal whose cowardice has set the pattern for centuries to come. Instead of employing science to benefit mankind he has made it the servant of the arbitrary authority of the reactionary state.

Brecht portrays Galileo as a sensualist, for whom even the quest of knowledge is a pleasure of the senses. The representatives of the church are treated fairly: they are portrayed as clever, intelligent men who argue their case with skill. With a wealth of detail Brecht draws the characters of the daughter, the motherly housekeeper, and her son Andrea.

Galileo is a genius; he is also lecherous and gluttonous. His greatest sensual pleasure is the joy of discovery, whis is almost irrational. Not only does he falsely lay claim to the invention of the telescope, he also writes servile letters to the Medici; and he recants his theories. In an early version of the play Brecht excused Galileo for his recanting, but later changed this. Galileo is a criminal because he establishes the pattern of making the scientist subservient to the state, a situation that culminates in the production of the atom bomb. Galileo, the hero of science, is the embodiment of reason in all its splendor, ruined by the inability to overcome the baser side of his human nature.

Brecht portrays female characters with special skill. In his earlier plays he presents chiefly loose women, but in *Die heilige Johanna der Schlachthöfe* he introduces a new type of womanhood—the woman revolutionary.

Die heilige Johanna der Schlachthöfe is in part a parody of Schiller's *Die Jungfrau von Orleans*. Joan Dark, a simple girl belonging to the Black Straw Hats—a group modeled on the Salvation Army—tries to alleviate the sufferings of the workers in the Chicago stockyards. She learns that the prevailing unemployment is caused by the machinations of Pierpont Mauler, the canned-meat king, who is waging a life-and-death struggle with his competitors. Joan goes to his office and spots him at once, as St. Joan did the dauphin. Her pleas for the poor move him, but he tries to prove to her that the poor are wicked and not worthy of her efforts. Joan succeeds in driving the meat-packers out of the chapel of the Straw Hats, but she herself is expelled from the organization. She decides to share the sufferings of the unemployed.

Sent out by the communists to call a strike, she declines because violence is to be used. The strike fails; Mauler ruins his competitors and opens the factories. Joan, completely worn out, dies. With her last breath she proclaims that the world cannot be improved without violence. The meat-packers and the Black Straw Hats, who want to use the touching story of Joan's life for their own propaganda, drown her last words with pseudo-religious humbug by which she is canonized as the valiant little St. Joan of the Stockyards. Although a grotesquely naive picture of capitalistic society is presented, this is one of Brecht's best plays.

The motherly type of woman is presented in *Mutter Courage und ihre Kinder,* a chronicle of the Thirty Years' War, accompanied by music. Mother Courage is an itinerant who follows the Swedish and Imperial armies with her covered wagon, selling supplies to the soldiers. Each of her three children is from a different father: aggressive Eilif, slow but honest Schweizerkäs, and the mentally retarded daughter Katrin. Living by the war, Mother Courage must pay its due. She loses her children, one after another.

The honest Schweizerkäs is shot because he refuses to betray the hiding place of the regimental cashbox. Eilif is executed as a looter. Katrin, disfigured by lecherous soldiers, tries to save the town of Halle from attack. Having roused the townspeople with her drum, she is shot.

Mother Courage is left alone. Determined to continue her itinerant life, she wearily pulls her cart to catch up with the army. There are brilliantly drawn characters in the play: the Protestant chaplain, who escapes capture by disguising himself as Mother Courage's handyman; the Dutch cook, who lives with Mother Courage for a while and offers to marry her, but leaves when she insists on taking Katrin, her dumb daughter, with her; the harlot Yvette, who becomes the wealthy widow of an Austrian colonel.

Brecht insisted that Mother Courage is a negative character, a profiteer who sacrifices her children to her mercenary operations, but every audience is deeply moved by her fate. As in so many other of Brecht's plays, emotion and feeling overcome reason; Brecht's poetic sensitiveness is far deeper than his rationalistic aims. Although Mother Courage is burdened with greed and guilt, her basic human traits make her a sympathetic character. In the final analysis she is a truly heroic character since she maintains an unwavering affirmative attitude toward life, which has brought her only anguish and suffering.

Brecht treats the theme of motherliness very touchingly in the character of the servant girl in *Der kaukasische Kreidekreis*. It is based on the old Chinese play *The Circle of Chalk*. The first performance, in English, was given in Northfield, Minnesota, in 1948. It was not until 1954 that it was performed in German at the Theater am Schiffbauerdamm in Berlin.

In the prologue to the play, members of two collective farms in Soviet Georgia are in dispute over a tract of land. A folk singer, to bring out the ethical side of the situation, sings an old legend of the circle of chalk. This constitutes the play.

A rich governor and his wife and little son live in luxury. On

Easter Sunday morning, the governor is murdered by revolting barons. The widow flees, leaving her son behind. The child is saved by a kitchen maid, Grusche, who takes it into the mountains.

In order that the child may have a name, Grusche consents to marry a rich peasant who is apparently in the last stages of a fatal ailment. He is, however, only feigning illness to escape being recruited. After the wedding ceremonies he quickly revives. The war ends and Grusche's fiancé returns. He is incensed to find her married and evidently a mother. Before she can explain, soldiers seize the child, the governor's widow appears and claims it, and the case goes to court.

The soldiers have just hanged the judge. Amused by the jests of the drunken village scribe Azdak, who is under arrest for sheltering the Grand Duke, they put him on the bench. For two years he acts as judge, taking bribes, but favoring the poor and downtrodden. He is about to be hanged when the Grand Duke pardons him.

Again he sits as judge in the courtroom. He hears the case of the two women claiming the same child. Having listened to their pleas, he has a circle of chalk drawn and puts the child in the center. Each woman is to try and drag him out. The governor's widow pulls him out violently, but Grusche, worried about injuring the little one, does not use force. Azdak awards the child to Grusche, arguing that through her gentleness she showed the greater love. During the rejoicing that follows, Azdak disappears. The singing commentator summarizes the verdict by saying that things should "belong to those who are good for them: the children to those who are motherly . . . and the valley to those who will irrigate it and make it fruitful."

This is one of Brecht's greatest plays and an excellent example of the technique of the epic drama. The wicked characters are masked, the action is stylized, there are many musical and poetic interludes. In the character of the judge, Brecht presents a portrait of himself: simple and complex, servile and arrogant, shrewd and foolish, humble and conceited. Again instinct overcomes reason.

Brecht's poetic expressiveness and his deep human feelings

are shown no more effectively than in *Der gute Mensch von Sezuan*. Filled with lyric passages and much humor, its plot is fascinating and its message is profound. The lowly Chinese street-walker, with deepest motherly feelings and social consciousness, expresses an ethical and at the same time eminently practical view of life.

The music for this parable play set in modern China is by Paul Dessau. Three gods, who are quite human in their failings, have come to earth to look for a really good human being. Unless at least one can be found, the world cannot continue to exist. Weary from their fruitless search they enter the town of Setzuan. They ask Wang, the water-seller, to find them shelter for the night.

A number of townsmen are asked for lodging by Wang, but they all refuse to take these strangers into their homes. Only Shen Te, a prostitute, is ready to receive them. She even sends away a customer to keep her room free for them.

The grateful gods reward her with a gift of money in the morning. With this she buys a small tobacco shop. As soon as the neighbors hear of it, a horde of parasites, would-be relatives, and beggars descends upon her. To protect herself Shen Te assumes the role of a ruthless male cousin Shui Ta. This determined young man drives the unwelcome horde away. Inquirers for Shen Te are told that she is visiting in a distant town. When she returns, Shui Ta disappears. Shen Te continues her acts of kindness, distributing rice freely.

She saves a young air pilot, Yang Sun, from suicide and plans to marry him. He, however, only wants her money as a bribe to get a job as an airmail pilot. The wedding reception is a complete failure. Shen Te is about to lose her shop when Shui Ta reappears and takes over. He starts a tobacco factory and employs Yang Sun as the ruthless overseer. The protracted absences of Shen Te worry Wang, the water-carrier; he suspects that Shui Ta has murdered her. Shui Ta is arrested and brought to trial, and the three gods sit as judges. Accused of cruelty by a number of witnesses, Shui Ta suddenly removes his disguise and reveals that he is really Shen Te. Only by employing ruthlessness at times could the good woman manage to exist. The thought is expressed that the good cannot live in this world and remain good. The gods are greatly relieved that they have found one good human being, but they give Shen Te no aid when she appeals to them. Somehow, they say, she will manage; let her assume the ruthless role of her cousin once a month. The gods float away into heaven.

Although many of the incidents and remarks are highly amusing, they are often of deep significance. Wang begs the gods to relax the stricter divine injunctions for the sake of hard-pressed humanity. He suggests goodwill instead of love, fairness instead of justice, and decency instead of honor. The gods reject these, saying they would be harder to maintain. Shen Te summarizes the basic idea of the play in the words: "Something must be wrong with your world. Why is there a reward for wickedness, why do the good receive such hard punishment?"

Brecht yearned to be a writer for the common people, but his work is primarily appreciated by intellectuals. He wanted to serve the revolution; but he was rejected by professional communists because of his deep sympathy with the individual. He endeavored to arouse the critical faculties of his audience but moved them to tears. He sought to spread the cold light of reason but created a warm, poetic atmosphere and affirmed his faith in human nature.[7]

Anna Seghers   (born 1900)

Anna Seghers, whose real name is Netty Reiling, was born in Mainz in 1900, the daughter of a wealthy antique dealer. She was raised in comfort and never knew the poverty that she describes with such remarkable detail in her books. At the universities of Cologne and Heidelberg she studied the history of art, and wrote her doctor's thesis on "The Jew and Jewishness in the works of Rembrandt."

In 1925 she married the Hungarian writer Laszlo Radványi, who introduced her to communism. Her first literary efforts appeared in the *Frankfurter Zeitung*. In 1928 she adopted as her *nom de plume* Anna Seghers, the name of one of her heroines, and joined the Communist Party. With the advent of the Nazis in

1933, she and her husband fled to France and later to Mexico. In 1947 she returned to Germany, going to East Berlin.'

Anna Seghers was attracted to communism by emotional rather than intellectual considerations. On her sixtieth birthday she confessed that methodical thinking was foreign to her; intellectual processes to her were always something strange, erratic, and mysterious. This is shown in her books, where the emotional always dominates. For her, communism is not a philosophical system or a political program, but rather a matter of faith and feeling, of devotion to a noble cause. Intuition, not intellect, has always been her guide.

This is clearly revealed in the title story of her first book after joining the Communist Party, *Auf dem Weg zur amerikanischen Botschaft und andere Erzählungen* (1930; "on the way to the American embassy, and other stories"). The action takes place in Paris in 1927. A parade of demonstrators is on the way to the American Embassy to protest against the imminent execution of Sacco and Vanzetti. A stranger who has just arrived is caught up by chance in the procession. He sees the flags and signs, he hears the music and the songs. Although he does not know what it is all about, he instinctively marches along. Actually he would have preferred to sit down at a sidewalk café and look on. The whole scene exerts a mysterious, a powerful influence on him, and he is unable to distinguish the imagined from the real. Like a somnambulist he continues to march; he is so content that he resists the urge to wake up. When the police start shooting at the demonstrators, he yearns to sacrifice himself for the cause. He is struck by a bullet, topples over, and remains lying in the street.

Anna Seghers by no means condemns the irrational behavior of her hero; quite the contrary, she glorifies it. The lonely stranger by joining the march of demonstrators overcomes his individualism and experiences the delightful feeling of belonging to a community. It is not the instinct of gregariousness but rather the sense of solidarity– an emotion that is raised by Anna Seghers to almost religious intensity.

The anonymous individual who marches along ecstatically and is ready to make a senseless sacrifice is a type that appears later in many of Anna Seghers's books. She is fond of portraying

simple beings who think very little and feel very deeply, who
have an unshakable belief and never doubt. They are not capable
of judging accurately what is happening to them. The will power
of nearly all her heroes is overwhelmed by an unknown, powerful
force—a force that drives them to do unusual deeds, to bear
patiently unspeakable sufferings, and to make even the supreme
sacrifice.[1] The question of the reasonableness of the sacrifice is
never broached. Even where there is a complete failure, the death
of the martyr is a symbol of future triumph. One cannot help
thinking of the saying, "The blood of the martyrs is the seed of
the church."

This irrationality appears also in a longer narrative, *Der
Aufstand der Fischer von St. Barbara* (1928; The Revolt of the
Fishermen of St. Barbara). For this book Anna Seghers received
the Kleist Prize.

The fishermen of St. Barbara are being shamelessly exploited
by their employers. A revolutionary, Johann Hull, a mysterious,
erratic character, comes to their village. "He had only to clap his
hands and a revolt leaped out of him, into the city, across the
town, to the coast, perhaps across the frontier."

In a neighboring town, Hull had organized an uprising that
proved a failure. In St. Barbara he rouses the despairing fishermen to a revolt, which is cruelly suppressed by the police and the
military. A number of workers perish; nothing is accomplished.
Neither Hull's ability as an organizer nor the need for a revolt
are questioned at any time.

Anna Seghers transcends the momentary defeat by stressing
the everlasting and permanent factors of revolutionary action.
"But long after the soldiers had withdrawn and the fishermen
were out at sea, revolt still sat in the empty, white, and bare
summer market place and thought quietly of his own whom he
had born, raised, cared for, and protected, for that which was best
for them."

Anna Seghers at times uses highly symbolic and metaphorical
language. The entire narrative, in fact, is a mythology of social
revolt. The time of the action is not given, nor is the exact loca-
tion of St. Barbara indicated. The fact that the fishermen have
Scandinavian, Dutch, German, and English names is of no signifi-

cance. The wretched fishing village is a symbol; it might be anywhere at any time.

On the other hand, in the novel *Die Gefährten* (1932; "the companions") the time and the place are given. The action takes place between 1919 and 1929 in Poland, Hungary, and Bulgaria. The communist revolutionaries who want to change the world are tortured or murdered or forced to flee. Again, however, the background is not quite authentic, even though time and place are indicated. As in Anna Seghers's other novels, the milieu is merely the stage for the action carried through by universal types.

The story begins with the words, "Everything was over." The defeat of the communists is described. But as in her other works, Anna Seghers emphasizes the invincibility of the communist ideal. No matter what happens, the revolutionary spirit will survive; it will be transmitted by faithful followers and will triumph.

A young Polish worker, Janek, not bright but unswervingly loyal to the party, is locked up in a Warsaw prison. He meets another, older communist, Solonjenko, who places his hand reverently on his head. Janek is amazed; for the moment he does not realize that what is in the older man is also in him. Ten years later he is again incarcerated. In prison he meets a younger communist, Labiak, who admires his fortitude and humor. Janek, as Solonjenko did to him a decade ago, places his hand on Labiak's bare head, who is unaware "that the same strength was in him while Janek's hand rested on his head."

These gestures and actions, as well as the psychological attitudes of Anna Seghers's principal characters, have a mystical and religious air about them. The laying on of hands and the idea of the transmission of spiritual qualities are taken directly from the orthodox Christian ritual.[2]

The author's novels written in exile continue to picture the same type of unthinking, loyal individual. The hero of *Der Kopflohn* (1933; A Price on His Head) is a young, helpless German worker who has stabbed a police officer during a demonstration. He seeks refuge in the home of relatives in a little village, where he is finally exposed by a Nazi.

In *Der Weg durch den Februar* (1935; "the way through February") the unsuccessful uprising against the Dollfuss regime in Austria in February of 1934 is the setting. Again the hero is a simple-minded, awkward, common workingman, Willaschek, who is sometimes with the social-democrats and sometimes with the communists, not quite sure what the aims of either are. He is brought before the court, accused of having shot an officer during a street brawl. He is barely able to follow the proceedings. When he is condemned to twelve years in prison he cries out, "We will be the judges of tomorrow!" He goes to his cell, serene and quiet, "like the very strongest going through life." He is consoled by his women relatives, who will think of him at home and at work. "He knows his own and his own know him" ("Er kennt die Seinen und die Seinen kennen ihn"). These words are an almost literal quotation from the New Testament.

Invariably Anna Seghers's heroes are the lowly, the poor, and the slow-witted. Despite their obvious inability to cope with the problems they face, they have, like the ancient martyrs, a vision of future glory. They bring to mind the Biblical promise, "The meek shall inherit the earth."

To give one more example: in *Die Rettung* (1937; "the rescue") the sufferings of the coal miners in the years 1929–33 are described. The hero is not only simple-minded; he is a moody, erratic older man who for months occupies himself at home with the building of the model of a church out of matchsticks. Upon the accession to power of the Nazis he is persuaded to become a communist. Eager to take part in the resistance movement, he is a complete failure.

Many of the East German writers had little to offer in the way of originality in style in the beginning. The favorite format was that of the autobiographical novel or documentary report. Anna Seghers, however, employed the techniques she had learned in the West; there are evident influences of Joyce, Dos Passos, and Hemingway in her novels. The plain, realistic structure of her narratives is often embellished by lyrical and metaphorical passages in an almost expressionistic style. The atmosphere that she creates is not a cheerful one; bitterness, melancholy, and gloom predominate. Her simple-minded heroes face crises and disasters; they go through suffering, anguish, and fear.

When Anna Seghers joined the Communist Party she did so

with a firm conviction and an almost religious devotion. Her ideal was to serve the party with her writings; literature was to strengthen communism and gain victory for it. In the attempt to make the synthesis between art and propaganda she has not been too successful; the two do not mix well. In *Der Kopflohn, Die Rettung,* and *Der Weg durch den Februar* she tried to find an explanation for the failure of the communists in 1933. The party, however, was not interested in a critical analysis of its shortcomings. Adjusting her political thinking obediently, Anna Seghers reduced her criticism to very mild statements; for example, that the party had not been active enough immediately before Hitler's seizure of power.

She made even greater concessions after the Soviet Writers' Congress in Moscow in 1934 announced "socialist realism" as the new theory of art. Experimenting in art and literature was forbidden. Western writers such as Joyce, Proust, and Dos Passos were denounced.

Anna Seghers's attitude is revealed in her correspondence with the critic Georg Lukács. She was ready to accept socialist realism but vigorously opposed the idea of dropping experimenting. She argued that in every period of political or social upheaval art and literature have been characterized by marked ruptures in style and by experiments in the attempt to create something new. She is all for socialist realism and for the idea that literature must serve the party. But by restraining and restricting the writer, his effectiveness in spreading communist ideals is lessened if not entirely eliminated. Only the true artist can instil life and reality in his creations. But he must not be bound to a given period and a given society; he must be free to express himself, even in his more abstract moods. Merely adhering to socialist realism does not even guarantee loyalty to socialist ideals. Some communist authors have employed the style but have failed to express the proper thoughts. The party should by no means interfere with the author and prescribe the means of expression.[3]

Anna Seghers realized that she herself had yielded too much under the pressure of the party critics and had landed in a blind alley with her book *Rettung.* The fear of being accused of deviation had paralyzed her hand and had prevented her from achieving her best. She was determined, for the sake of her own integrity, and in behalf of the party, to rid herself of this fear and to express the truth as she saw it.

Her outstanding novel, *Das siebte Kreuz* (1946; The Seventh Cross, 1942), at which she worked from 1937 to 1940, was written under the most depressing international and personal circumstances. The Civil War in Spain had ended with the defeat of the Republicans; Stalin cruelly purged his opponents; the trials in Moscow shocked even the communists outside Russia; tens of thousands were exiled; Stalin made a pact with Hitler, who had seized Czechoslovakia and Austria; Poland was invaded by German armies; France interned German anti-Nazis, among them the husband of Anna Seghers, who remained in Paris with her two small children.

Amid these depressing circumstances Anna Seghers wrote *Das siebte Kreuz*. Portraying life in Germany in 1937, it was to be a polemic against National Socialism. It turned out to be, however, a deeply touching and moving story of a devoted radical who flees the Nazi terror. Instead of promoting hate and hostility the book preaches pity and love. Its basic thought is expressed in the words, "Mercy instead of justice."

Seven communists escape from a concentration camp. Six are recaptured and crucified; the seventh cross remains empty. This was intended for Georg Heisler, who succeeds in escaping. Like other modest heroes portrayed by Anna Seghers, Heisler is a simple-minded chap who became a communist chiefly through his interest in sports. Anything but intellectual, he smilingly rejected the reading material offered him. Emotionally and intuitively he was loyal and fearless; the party relied on him in situations that required daring.

Like a hunted animal he drifts from town to town in the Rhine valley, helped by kind and sympathetic people. Some of the incidents are profoundly moving, especially the description of the night that Heisler spends in the Mayence cathedral. Gazing at the stained glass windows, illuminated by lamps and candles flickering in the semidarkness, he lets his thoughts wander: "Yes, that must be those two who were chased out of paradise. . . . Yes, those must be the heads of the cows looking into the manger where the child lay for whom there was no room in the inn. Yes, that must be the Last Supper, when he already knew that he was betrayed; yes, that must be the soldier who struck him with the lance as he hung on the cross. . . ."

Like so many of Anna Seghers's heroes, Heisler is a modest, unassuming individual whose attachment to communism is conditioned by his unwavering faith and deep feeling. Strangely enough, the term "communist" is not even used with reference to him. Throughout the book he plays the role of the pursued fugitive. Worn out and fatigued, ill and hungry, plagued by fearful dreams and memories of the concentration camp, fluctuating between hope and despair, he makes his way along the Rhine and the Main.

This landscape, the native region of the author, and its inhabitants are described vividly and affectionately. Other communist writers generally draw a dismal picture of life in the Third Reich. Anna Seghers, on the other hand, stresses the pleasanter aspects of the everyday life of the common people.

Heisler is helped by former members of the party and also by others who have no particular political leanings. There are, for example, the Jewish doctor who bandages his hand, the seamstress who supplies him with fresh clothing, the gardener's apprentice who misleads the Gestapo with false clues, and his former wife, Eli, and Paul Röder, the friend of his youth. The latter never wanted to have anything to do with communism. It is he who risks everything to save Georg and plays the decisive role in the final successful escape to Holland.

What is significant about all the help that Georg is given is that both the communists and the anti-Nazis who aid him do so as a matter of decency and personal kindness, and not at the behest of the party. The resistance to the Nazi terror is not motivated politically but is a question of conscience and ethics. The record of Georg Heisler's escape is a passion story. Its central theme is the integrity and rectitude of the average person. It does not involve the reader in any political ideology. This is expressed in the final sentence of the book: "We all felt how powerfully and fearfully external forces may reach into a man, into his innermost being, but we also felt that there was something in his innermost recesses which was unassailable and inviolable."

Anna Seghers displays unusual artistry in her descriptions of the Rhine Valley and its people, which undoubtedly recalled many fond memories of her own childhood and youth in that area. In giving her imagination free reign, she disregarded any possible concerns about ideology. With much skill she was able to portray realistically a poetic vision.

In her next novel, *Transit* (1943), she did just the opposite: she transformed a real and concrete world into a poetic vision. When the German armies approached Paris in May, 1940, Anna Seghers fled to Marseilles, where she wrote the novel and where the action takes place. Based on personal experiences, the novel is essentially autobiographical. Described is the struggle of despairing refugees in their efforts to obtain visas and passports (*"transit"*), and their constant confrontation with a complicated and matter-of-fact bureaucracy. The situation is so hopeless that even Anna Seghers begins to lose faith. The only thing that sustains her is a presentiment of her own indestructability. Even reality loses its substance; it seems unintelligible. It cannot be depicted realistically. Life is like a nightmare: the feverish activity of the city crowded with refugees is a symbol of the absurdity of existence to which the hapless individual is delivered.

East German critics were disturbed by the book. They did not like the comparison of reality to a nightmare and the stress on the irrationality of existence. It seemed related to the *Weltanschauung* of Franz Kafka. The East German official literary guide commented that undoubtedly the author, when she wrote the novel, was suffering from the same psychological depression as the hero of the book.

The novel was not in Anna Seghers's characteristic manner; it was practically existentialist. She recovered her usual point of view, however, soon thereafter. With the aid of the League of American Authors she left Marseilles and went to Mexico where a number of communist writers in exile had formed a colony. Her new surroundings influenced her thinking. She rewrote the final chapters of *Transit*, so that the book closes on a highly optimistic note.

After countless difficulties the narrator obtains the necessary travel papers, but then he declines to flee. Instead he decides to remain and help the French fight the Nazis. The mystical, religious thought is expressed that even if one bleeds to death in this familiar soil, something of one will continue to grow, like the bushes and the trees that the invaders have tried to uproot. The same spiritual aura is cast over the story *"Post ins gelobte Land"* ("mail to the promised land"), which is set in a Jewish milieu, partly in Palestine. Significantly, it is not included in her collected works published in East Berlin (1951–53).

In Mexico Anna Seghers wrote the novel *Der Ausflug der toten Mädchen* (1947; "excursion of the dead girls"), which is characterized by an unusual parallelism in structure. Into the description of a happy school-outing of a group of girls, Anna Seghers blends the destiny that is to be the lot of each of the pupils and the teacher many years later during the Third Reich. There is a continual flow, backward and forward, between the time of World War I and II, between the past and the present, between dream and reality.

Upon her return from Mexico Anna Seghers revised her novel *Die Toten bleiben jung* (The Dead Stay Young) which was published in 1949. It is typical of her later writing in East Germany.

At the Congress of Authors of the German Democratic Republic held in January 1956 she said:

No gripping action is thinkable without conflicts. All books that move people do so through the conflicts within the plot. . . . Only in a conflict can the individual reveal his character and all his private and social relationships. . . . In our books too often there is no genuine conflict, only a pseudo-conflict . . . since no character is tested and forced to make decisions. The persons in the story seem to be provided with placards like angels and devils in a medieval mystery play. . . .

But the approach she criticized is the very one she uses in *Die Toten bleiben jung*. Here she proposed to present a comprehensive picture of political conditions in Germany between 1919 and 1945 and to describe the destinies of representatives of the various strata and classes of society. In the first chapter, during the street fights in Berlin in January of 1919, four men, three officers and a soldier, murder a young revolutionary worker while he is removing rubbish. The murderers and the girl friend of the victim are the main persons in the five biographical narratives into which the book is divided. There are no real conflicts; there is no character development. The industrialists, Prussian officers, Baltic barons, peasants, social-democratic workers, and communist functionaries are all stereotypes. Their actions are not motivated by inner convictions; they perform to illustrate trite political and sociological ideas. All is black and white. The anti-communists are invariably cynical scoundrels; the leftists are all fearless, inspired idealists.

But in this novel, too, Anna Seghers resorts to a mystical symbolism to express some of her basic notions, such as the continuity and indestructibility of the revolution. After the death of the murdered worker, his fiancée gives birth to a boy who is named Hans. Although he knows nothing of his father and is given no political orientation, he carries on the revolutionary traditions of his father. When he is thirteen, he joins the Hitler Youth, ostensibly to enlighten his comrades about the evils of the Nazi regime. Toward the end of World War II he is shot as an anti-Nazi by the same officer Wenzlow, who had murdered his father. Hans resembles his father so closely that the officer for a moment believes the revolutionary of 1919 has been resurrected. Like his father, Hans has a girl friend, who also gives birth to a child after his death. The revolution must live on!

Despite this almost grotesque symbolism, there are fine passages and well-drawn characters in the book, especially that of the mother of Hans. This novel is the last one that is worthy of Anna Seghers's literary gift. All her books written after the founding of the German Democratic Republic are so inferior, that they seem to be written for readers of limited intelligence or for children. The effort to indoctrinate is so obvious that the literary values are negligible.

In the story "Die Rückkehr" (1949; "the return") a worker leaves the Russian Zone after World War II, spends some time in West Germany, is deeply disappointed, and returns to the wonderful "Democratic Republic." In a longer narrative, *Der Mann und sein Name* (1952; "the man and his name"), a former SS-member frees himself of the stigma of his past and after various complications becomes a model citizen of East Germany. In the story "Vierzig Jahre der Margarete Wolf" ("forty years of Margaret Wolf") an old woman gives an account of the fate of her relatives since World War I.

The novel *Die Entscheidung* (1959; "the decision") presents a vast panorama. The book runs to 600 pages. More than 150 different characters appear; the action takes place in East Germany, West Germany, France, and the United States. The majority of the characters are the same stereotypes encountered in the novels of the average East German writer. There are the honest, reliable worker who criticises life in East Germany but is a loyal communist at heart; the hesitant bourgeois intellectual who overcomes his prejudices and finally cooperates enthusiastically in building up the socialist state; the eager engineer who is exposed as an American agent or as a former member of the Gestapo; the conscientious woman worker who informs on her neighbor; the youth whose parents perished in the war and who now finds his family in the life of the community; the wise and indefatigable party secretary who appears at the right moment as the rescuing angel; and the West German factory owner who drinks cognac and has diabolic designs on East Germany.

Die Entscheidung demonstrates the complete capitulation of Anna Seghers to the party and the collapse of a great talent. She is a classic example of the very errors she denounced at the Authors' Congress in 1956, when she warned against the overstress on political ideology and the use of stereotypes.

The scholastic style is poison, no matter how Marxistic it tries to behave. . . . For it results in stultification instead of action. . . . There is no excitement for the reader in such books. He does not have to strain his thought processes, for he knows the pattern on which the book is modeled in advance just as well as the author.[4]

This is the very level to which Anna Seghers has sunk.

Bruno Apitz   (born 1900)

Of the many East German books about Nazi concentration camps, the classic is undoubtedly *Nackt unter Wölfen* (1958; "naked among wolves"). The author, Bruno Apitz, wrote it from personal experience, for he spent many years in prisons and camps. Through the writing of this book the unknown party functionary and composer of mediocre radio plays (*Hörspiele*) moved into the front ranks of East German writers. Within two years the book reached a circulation of half a million copies in East Germany. It was translated into twenty-two languages, achieved a West German edition in Hamburg, and was filmed, turned into a play, and produced on television and radio. The screen version was shown in New York in 1967.

Bruno Apitz, born in 1900 in Leipzig, was the twelfth child of a linoleum printer and a laundress. He showed radical leanings quite early. At seventeen he was imprisoned for carrying on antiwar propaganda. In 1927 he joined the Communist Party. For nine years he sat in a jail in Waldheim and later he spent eight years in Buchenwald. His incarceration in that notorious concentration camp gave him the material for *Nackt unter Wölfen*.

The action takes place in the spring of 1945 in the stockade located on the lovely wooded heights above Weimar where Goethe used to stroll. There is unusual excitement, for every official radio message of the Reichswehr (the German army) announces the steady approach of the American Army. The officers and SS-men are planning to flee. The prisoners have organized an elaborate secret resistance movement.

This is the backdrop for a touching human drama. A Jewish prisoner arriving from Auschwitz brings a ragged valise into camp in which is cramped a half-starved three-year-old Polish orphan whose parents were murdered by the Nazis. Despite the threat of instant death that the discovery of the child might bring them, all of the prisoners pledge their lives for the safety of the urchin. They feed him, nurse him, conceal him, and save him a half dozen times at a hair's breath. The efforts of the SS-men to

get the youngster fail. The child becomes the symbol of the resistance of helpless humanity in the face of brutal barbarism. Just as
in Anna Seghers's *Das siebte Kreuz*, the men do not act for political or ideological reasons but are motivated entirely by kindness
and purely human feelings. The Nazis flee, the Americans arrive,
and the child is triumphantly borne from the camp on the arms
of one of the resistance leaders.

Apitz displays ability in building up dramatic situations. He
also shows considerable skill in describing the psychological reactions of the various SS-officers, as well as those of the outstanding
prisoners.

The critic Reich-Ranicki, who grants this in part, sneers at
the likelihood of hard-boiled conspirators, particularly communists, being capable of any humane feelings. He rejects the idea
that they would be ready to risk their lives to save a Jewish
infant. Anderle, another West German commentator, however, is
more generous; he believes that even communists can be kind and
generous. Apitz sounds the same warning as Anna Seghers: the
unity of communism must not exclude the purely human; it must
not eliminate the individual.

The little Polish child who escaped the Nazi terror in
Buchenwald was a real human being. Apitz, who was deeply interested in learning what happened to him later on, found him
after a lengthy search. Juschu had grown into a healthy, promising young man, whose name was Stefan Jerzy Zweig. Together, in
1964, they visited the former concentration camp at Buchenwald.

Throughout his narrative Apitz is generally matter-of-fact;
he rarely indulges in sentiment or emotion, even when the situation becomes tense. The final release of the prisoners and their
bursting forth from the camp is described in a paragraph of seven
lines:

Men laughed, wept, danced. They sprang on the tables, threw their
arms high into the air, screamed at one another, screamed, screamed as
if madness had taken hold of them. They could no longer be held back.
Out of all the blocks they burst forth. Everyone dashed out, and like a
whipped-up stormy wave, the intoxicated mass flooded the paradeground.

And the final lines:

Like a nutshell, the child swayed above the waving heads. In the crush it was whisked through the narrow gate, and then the stream tore it along on its released torrents that could no longer be contained.

Aptiz has written nothing worthy of mention since 1958.

Franz Karl Weiskopf (1900–55)

F. K. Weiskopf was born in 1900 in Prague, the son of an official. A member of the Austrian army during World War I, he returned to Czechoslovakia after the cessation of hostilities and edited a workers' illustrated paper. In 1928 he settled in Germany. When the situation became too perilous in Europe, he left for New York. There he was cordially received as a representative of the Czech resistance forces.

After World War II, Weiskopf was a diplomat in Czechoslovakia for a number of years and was sent to Washington as a counselor in the Czech Embassy. Finally he settled in East Berlin.

Being very fastidious about expressing himself in the best possible German, he wrote and rewrote his novels, even changing their titles. He wrote a good account of the German authors who were in exile, entitled *Unter fremden Himmeln* (1949; "under foreign skies").

Weiskopf's major work, however, is a novel entitled *Die Versuchung* (1937; "the temptation"), which was republished in a revised edition in 1954 as *Lissy oder die Versuchung* ("Lissy, or the temptation").

The leading character is Lissy Schroeder. Her father is a foreman in a factory; she works in a Berlin department store, where she sells cigarettes. She is discharged when her employers become aware that she is pregnant. Because of the economic depression, she cannot obtain employment. She marries Fromeyer, an employee in a travel agency. He also loses his job. He joins a Nazi organization and prospers. After the establishment of the Third Reich, he lives in wealth and comfort. Lissy, whose sympathies are with the workers, finds herself in a dilemma. She helps Max Franke, a communist, who has to hide from the Nazis. Lissy leaves Fromeyer; she finds her happiness in the working-class movement.

In 1923 Weiskopf published a volume of poems entitled *Es geht eine Trommel* ("a drum is sounding"). His travels in the Soviet Union are recorded in *Umsteigen ins 21. Jahrhundert* (1927; "transfer to the 21st century") and *Zukunft im Rohbau* (1932; "future in rough construction").

These reports are well done, since Weiskopf is a keen observer. His novels and his poems are not highly regarded. On the other hand, he established a reputation as writer of anecdotes, specially in his *Anekdotenbuch* (1954; "book of anecdotes").

As a former citizen of the Austro-Hungarian Monarchy, Weiskopf was interested in its decline and described this in a series of novels: *Abschied vom Frieden* (1948; "farewell to peace"); *Inmitten des Stromes* (1950; "in the middle of the stream"); and *Welt in Wehen* (1955; "world in travail").

Willi Bredel *(born 1901)*

Willi Bredel is one of the most successful authors of proletarian origin. He was a "writer-worker" forty years before the Bitterfeld Conference of 1959 developed that concept.

He was born in 1901 in Hamburg, the son of a tobacco worker. As a metal worker he was politically active from his youth. At the age of sixteen he was already an avowed communist; in 1919 he joined the party. For his participation in the October uprising in Hamburg (1923), he was condemned to two years in jail. There he began his literary activity, writing a brochure entitled *Mara, der Volksfreund* (1924; "Mara, friend of the people"). After his release he went to sea and visited Spain, Portugal, Italy, and North Africa.

In 1928 he again worked as a lathe-hand. Through his success in writing he was given a position as editor on the *Hamburger Volkszeitung*. His radical utterances led to his being condemned for "literary high treason" in 1930. During his prison term of two

years in a fortress, he wrote the novels *Maschinenfabrik N & K*
(1930; "machine factory N & K") and *Rosenhofstraße* (1931;
"rosecourt street").

In 1933 the Nazis sent him to the concentration camp in
Fuhlsbüttel, a suburb of Hamburg. With his rugged constitution
he was able to survive thirteen months of imprisonment, eleven of
them in solitary confinement and seven weeks in dark confinement. Bredel describes these harrowing experiences in his novel
Die Prüfung (1934; "the test"), which he wrote in four weeks in
Prague where he sought refuge after his release. His intention was
to present a documentary account of the cruelties perpetrated in
the Nazi concentration camps. His account is a remarkably fair
one; Bredel overlooks neither the deeper feelings of the execu-
tioners nor the human weaknesses of their victims. The leading
communist characters are portrayed as fighters rather than as passive victims. The terror could not break them; they passed the
test.

The novel *Dein unbekannter Bruder* (1937; "your unknown
brother") and the short story *Der Spitzel* (1936; "the informer")
are also descriptions of the concentration camps and the underground resistance to the terror in Nazi Germany.

Together with Brecht and Feuchtwanger, Bredel edited the
anti-Nazi journal *Das Wort* while he was in Moscow (1934).
There he also joined the National Committee Freies Deutschland.

From 1937 to 1939 Bredel was a commissar in the International Brigade in the Spanish Civil War. He describes his military
experiences in *Begegnung am Ebro* (1939; "encounter at the
Ebro"). It is done in bright colors; the tone is cheerful. Despite
all his severe sufferings in prisons and concentration camps,
Bredel remains an incurable optimist.

Considered his major work by the East German critics is his
novel in three volumes *Verwandte und Bekannte* ("relatives and
acquaintances"). It comprises *Die Väter* (1943; "the fathers"),
Die Söhne (1949; "the sons"), and *Die Enkel* (1953; "the grand-
children"). This series describes the fortunes of a worker's family
in Hamburg.

Since 1949 Bredel has written many short stories, sketches,
and documentary articles. He was twice awarded the National

Prize. The University of Rostock gave him an honorary doctor's degree.

Bodo Uhse   (1904–63)

Uhse's dream was a righteous Germany. In his youth he sought its realization through National Socialism, later through communism. He was a grim fighter, a tired optimist, a saddened enthusiast, and an embittered idealist.

Bodo Uhse was born in 1904 in Glogau on the Oder, eastern Germany, where he grew up. He entered the Hitler Youth in his boyhood and joined the National Socialist Party in 1923. The son of a former officer in Kaiser Wilhelm's army, Bodo Uhse was well acquainted with the German military milieu.

He began his journalistic career in Bamberg in Bavaria; later he became the editor of a Nazi paper in Ingolstadt, also in Bavaria. When a second Nazi daily was established in 1929, Bodo Uhse was put in charge. Despite his youth, he was already known as one of the most radical and gifted journalists. Very soon, however, he ran into difficulties with some of the highest Nazi leaders, including Hitler and Rosenberg, because of the socialistic ideas that he expressed in his articles. The Führer's ire was roused. In 1930 Uhse was expelled from the Nazi party.

Two years later he joined the communists, and in 1933 he fled to France. His first book, which appeared in Paris and Moscow in 1935, was entitled *Söldner und Soldat* ("mercenary and soldier"). In it he tells the story of his political development in the Germany of the 1920s. He stresses the idea that he wanted to be a soldier of the revolution, not just a mercenary.

During the civil war in Spain he was a commissar in the International Division (1936) after having worked at a Republican radio station. Later, in 1940, he went to Mexico, where he remained for the duration of World War II. In 1948 he returned to Germany.

Bodo Uhse's writing is uneven, containing many contradictory elements. His characters are rather pale and often not convincing; many of the plots are awkwardly constructed. He was skillful, however, in building up an atmosphere or a mood. There is a strange dichotomy in his narratives that alternates between coolness and passion, discipline and disorder, the simple and the complex, sensitivity and brutality. Throughout his career he was troubled by the search for an answer to the question, "Why?"

He introduces this exploratory attitude in his novel of the Spanish Civil War, *Leutnant Bertram* (1944; Lieutenant Bertram). Two young Germans face one another at the Spanish front: Sommerwand, a communist, a member of the International Brigade, and Bertram, who had been a flier in Hitler's Legion Condor, sent to Spain to fight against the Republicans.

In answer to Bertram's questioning and doubtful attitude, Sommerwand says:

"Listen, Bertram, when you were a child and as your consciousness awoke, did you ask: Why? Later you were sent in to a rough school and there they made you lose the habit of always asking that question. With us here it's different. We have never dropped these children's questions. We still ask after every horror: Why? We ask ourselves and others. And we won't rest until we find the answer."

Uhse began his novel in 1935 and finished it in 1943. The first part is set in a small town in northern Germany; only the second part deals with the Spanish Civil War. Uhse is quite objective in portraying the fighters on both sides, i.e., the professional officers of the Legion Condor and the amateur officers of the International Brigade, the Nazis and the communists. It is not the usual stereotype of white and black, as in so many socialist books.

Uhse brings out his own personal tragedy in this novel. Sometimes he becomes quite bitter.

The book was not a success. Unable to be either naively believing or sharply cynical, Uhse spread himself over the problematical and questionable and became diffuse and vague. He boldly approached questions precarious for a communist and then evaded answering them. His inhibitions, it is evident, constantly restrained him. Nevertheless, there are some well written chapters in the book that bring out his deep hatred of the Nazis, the sufferings of the refugees, the illusions of the communists, and the consciousness of guilt on the part of the Germans.

Upon his return to East Germany, Uhse faced the same problem of so many writers who had published books before the establishment of East Germany; namely, that of combining good writing and sincerity with effective propaganda in the officially approved style. Like others, Uhse failed.

His novel *Die Patrioten* (1954; "the patriots") describes the activities of two anti-Nazi resistance groups whose members have returned to Germany illegally from the Soviet Union. They are to organize underground fighters. Despite the fact that the novel is heavy, sterile, and boring, it received the National Prize.

The narrative broke off suddenly; a continuation was promised. Several deadlines were set and moved forward. Uhse was given a vacation from Berlin to work on it. All in vain—Uhse was unable to write a sequel.

Instead he collected stories and articles he had written while in exile. In 1949 he was made editor of *Aufbau*, a leading literary magazine. He took his job seriously and tried to raise the tone of this fairly liberal publication. His favorable reviews, however, of such officially disapproved authors as Hemingway and Sartre led to his dismissal in 1958.

In his various essays and articles he showed that he had maintained good taste and literary standards, independent of those of the official stereotypes. Once more, in January of 1963, he was appointed an editor, this time of *Sinn und Form*. He was able to publish only two issues, for he died six months later.

His career may be summed up in this quotation from his novel *Leutenant Bertram*: "Es bleibt eine Last ein Deutscher zu sein. Große Träume und böse Wirklichkeit, das ist Deutschland" ("It remains a burden to be a German. Grand dreams and evil realities, that is Germany.")

Eduard Claudius *(born 1911)*

Eduard Claudius is the pseudonym of Eduard Schmidt, who was born in Gelsenkirchen-Buer in 1911, the son of a construction worker. He entered the building trade as a bricklayer's apprentice. One day he was kicked off the scaffolding by the irate foreman. Claudius thought this incident ought to be brought to the attention of the union. So he sat down and wrote an article about it. The editor of the union bulletin rejected the manuscript, but the communistic *Ruhrecho* accepted it and printed it. This was Claudius' debut as an author.

In 1929 he set out on a tour of Europe and for three years he wandered through Italy, Austria, France, Spain, and Switzerland. In 1932 he returned and joined the Communist Party. Two years later he returned to Switzerland. He was arrested and jailed for a while. In 1936 he was again interned and was to be turned over to German officials. The Swiss police guard, however, who took him to the border let him escape. Claudius went to Spain, where he fought in the International Brigade and was wounded twice. After the civil war he went to France and then to Switzerland, where he was again arrested. Through Hermann Hesse's intervention he was saved from being turned over to the Nazis.

While in Switzerland he wrote the novella *Das Opfer* (1938; "the sacrifice"), which was published in the magazine *Das Wort*. In the internment camp he wrote his novel about the Spanish Civil War, *Grüne Oliven und nackte Berge* (Green Olives and Bare Mountains), which appeared in Zurich in 1945.

The plot, which is based on personal experiences, is simple enough. Jak, the hero, is wounded but returns to the front line trenches. Disillusioned, he asks himself, "Is it worthwhile to die for what has passed away?" After being permanently incapacitated for combat, Jak goes to Paris, where he meets his former love Thea. At first she begs him to make an effort to reenter middle-class life but then changes her attitude and severs her connection with her own past.

As a loyal communist Claudius did not fail to inject propaganda into his novel, but on the whole he presents a truthful and objective picture of the Spanish Civil War. The novel is in sharp contrast to Bredel's jaunty and optimistic account, *Begegnung am Ebro* (1938; "encounter at the Ebro"). East German critics were deeply disturbed by Claudius's book because of what it revealed. In several of the satellite states it was not published.

On the whole, the East German writers, in their portrayal of the war in Spain, aimed to stress the humanity rather than the military prowess of their heroes. Claudius does this in the following passage, which is one of several expressing the same thought.

"We communists are also human beings," Samuel remarked calm and sure. "But the tests that we have to undergo . . ." ". . . we will pass," interrupted a bright young voice, "for in us is the awareness of what is to be done. Feelings of horror run down the back of a communist with a cold shiver just as often. He is a human being like anyone else, but in getting rid of his fear, in that he shows that he is . . . a communist." . . . "Yes," said the young clear voice, "just because he is a human being, because he is a communist."

Claudius is a daring adventurer, temperamental and irascible, ambitious and fanatic. This is reflected in his prose style. He likes to portray elementary passions—burning hatred, inordinate love, and primitive fear. He claims that he was greatly influenced by Soviet literature, but the fact is that his later novels show American influence, especially *Haß* (1947; "hate") and *Gewitter* (1948; "storm"). His *Grüne Oliven und nackte Berge* is quite definitely modeled after the writing of Malraux and Hemingway. *Grüne Oliven und nackte Berge* is his best novel; he has not been able to equal it.

His second, longer work, *Menschen an unserer Seite* (1951; "people on our side"), is a superficial novel of propaganda in which the hero is an elderly worker whose dedicated service exerts an ideological influence on other members of the factory staff. Despite this, Claudius was criticized by the critics because he portrayed an ineffective party secretary, indicated all kinds of shortcomings in East Germany, and created his protagonist as a crude alcoholic. At first one of the state publishers refused to print the novel; later it was published and even awarded the National Prize.

In 1957 Claudius published a novel entitled *Von der Liebe soll man nicht nur sprechen* ("of love one should not just speak"). This book was a proletarian novel of character development between 1945 and 1953. It was a failure as party literature. It tells the story of a peasant girl, Christine, who first has an affair with a wealthy peasant, Hülsenbeck, but later goes over to Thonke, the party secretary. The critics were severe in condemning the book; they were especially outraged by the stress on the erotic.

Despite the unfavorable reviews, the book was put on school reading lists. The educators were more generous than the literary critics. According to their view: "The love between Christine and Thonke presents the maturation of new relationships, of a higher socialistic morality. . . . Matrimony is not a union based merely on sensual or economic considerations; it develops into an inwardly grounded companionship." The author tries to show that badly formed love relationships, which are dominated solely by sex, can develop into meaningful relationships.

Claudius became a little difficult in the eyes of the East German critics. He was, however, a loyal communist who had rendered valuable service to the party. As a reward he was given several diplomatic posts. From 1956 to 1959 he served as Consul General of East Germany in Syria, and later as Ambassador in Vietnam. These assignments in the Far East cause the suspicion to arise that they were put through by those who wanted to get rid of him tactfully, or that the annoyed author was glad to get away from the turgid atmosphere of East Berlin.

Claudius became deeply interested in the culture of southeastern Asia and began writing about it. In 1961 he published *Als die Fische die Sterne schluckten* ("when the fish swallowed the stars"), a collection of legends and fairy-tales of Vietnam, Laos, and Cambodia. East German critics praised his presentation of carefully observed details of Oriental life, but deplored his "false exotic romanticism." By this they meant his poetic descriptions of the love affairs of the girl Soft Cloud, the heroine of one of his stories.

Interesting as it is, the volume of fairy-tales and legends, written over a period of five years, seems a meager output for an author of his ability. Since then he has published nothing of note.

Erwin Strittmatter *(born 1912)*

Erwin Strittmatter occupies a high rank in the hierarchy of East German writers. In the official *Deutsche Literaturgeschichte* it says that "in the realistic representation of the life and struggle of the peasant, especially after 1945, Erwin Strittmatter has made the most significant artistic contribution. Erwin Strittmatter is today one of the leading writers of East Germany."

Strittmatter was born August 14, 1912, in Spremberg and spent his childhood in a little Silesian village. Like his father, he became a baker, working later as waiter, animal keeper, chauffeur, and handyman. Although he is celebrated as one of the proletarian writers, he was really a bourgeois and in his youth saw the problems of the worker from the middle-class point of view. This is evident every time he describes the comfortable life of the burger. It is interesting to note that the hero of what is considered his best book, i.e., *Der Wundertäter* (1957; "the wonder worker"), is the son of a cottager whose career is that of a "little man" during the first half of the century.

Strittmatter received little formal education, being largely self-taught. He joined a Socialist Working Youth group. He deserted from the army shortly before the end of hostilities in World War II. After 1945 he continued working as a baker, but also became active as a writer. He had some political experience, serving as a councilman in seven different communities. His earliest literary productions were short stories, sketches, and reports.

His first novel, *Der Ochsenkutscher* ("the ox-coachman"), appeared in 1950. It describes the childhood and youth of Gottlieb Kleineman, a young farm laborer. Lope, as he is called, has to work on the estate after leaving school. Later he finds employment in a nearby mine. After a short time he is discharged because a pamphlet by Friedrich Engels is found in his possession. Upon assumption of power by the Nazis, he leaves the village together with a former coachman and revolutionary worker. Through him Lope is guided into serious, active participation in the class struggle.

In 1953 Strittmatter published *Eine Mauer fällt* ("a wall falls"), a collection of short stories describing individual destinies in the struggle for the socialization of a village.

With the aid of Bertolt Brecht, Strittmatter's first play, *Katzgraben* (1954; "cat alley"), was produced by the Berlin Ensemble. Evidently Brecht, who was such an ingrained city-dweller and knew nothing of the country, was impressed by Strittmatter's colorful descriptions of life in a rural village. He also liked Strittmatter's simple, folksy language. By shaping Strittmatter's clumsy dramatic effort into a viable stage production, Brecht may have felt that this was a good opportunity for proving to the party that he was ready to follow their wishes, if not as an author, then at least as a theater director. After extensive and weary revisions, in which a staff of assistants took part, a drama resulted. The structure and the characters are obviously Brecht's contribution; the basic action and the language are Strittmatter's.

Although it secured the National Prize, it was not too successful. Some of the East German critics were severe in their comments. Brecht, however, had fulfilled his mission; he had helped a young and aspiring author.

The language of the play is so simple and clear, and deals with such everyday farm concerns, that even the dullest peasant can follow it. In one scene a party secretary points out the usefulness of the tractor to the backward rustics:

> Ox! Ox! Ox!
> Is such an animal the center of the world?
> Do think of it, we are now creating work levels
> Where one can borrow a tractor,
> And you, you cling to ox tails.
> Why not draw furrows with your nose?
> An ox can only be an expedient for us,
> A relief for the cow, as long as tractors are missing.
> Last year you saw only oxen; the party
> Has long since seen the tractor do the plowing.

In another play, *Die Holländerbraut* (1959; "the Holland bride"), Strittmatter describes social and political conditions in his native region, shortly before and shortly after the end of

World War II. This work is solely his; it shows that he possesses very little dramatic ability.

The heroine is the farm-worker Hanna Tainz, who is in love with the Nazi lieutenant Erdmann, the son of a wealthy peasant. She does not realize the depravity of the man she once adored, even after she becomes the mayor of the little village after the war. The noble-spirited members of the party however, help her to overcome her inner conflicts—for her own peace of mind and in the interest of the community.

Strittmatter's forte, however, is the prose narrative. He is at his best as an original popular story-teller who has humor and imagination. He is a keen observer; he is able to build up a village milieu with a few deft strokes. Occasionally he introduces a few satiric notes. The dialogues are colorful and true to life. When he attempts to become poetic, however, his metaphors are not very happy ones; often, they are ludicrous.

Many of the episodes in his novels are shallow and flat. Most striking is the intellectual poverty of his writings. His characters are predominantly stereotypes. To make doubly sure of their being identified correctly, he gives them significant names, like signboards (e.g., Gottlieb Kleineman, which means "God-loving little man"). He combines family names with *klein, groß,* and *mittel.* A factory owner is named Drückauf ("press hard"), a professor, Obenhin ("superficial"), and a club member, Hohlwind ("empty wind"). He overdoes this use of labels until it becomes absurd.

The world is usually observed from the point of view of a rather immature, naive, and intellectually limited hero. In *Der Ochsenkutscher,* for example, the poor, dreamy, seventeen-year-old village boy still speaks like a child. In this novel the personal elements predominate; the political aspect appears only incidentally.

In *Tinko,* however, published in 1954, the ideological is stressed. Strittmatter endeavors to show what changes have taken place in a village in the years of 1948 and 1949. The hero is an eleven-year-old boy, who is being brought up by his grandfather, a peasant of the old school. Of course, the grandfather is reactionary, arbitrary, and crafty. Suddenly the representative of progress appears—as in so many novels, a plain soldier who returns home after having been converted into an ardent communist in a Soviet prison camp.

In this case it is Tinko's father. The good, progressive younger man confronts the bad, reactionary old grandfather. The overcoming of the horrible past is symbolized by the death of the old man. Tinko, who tells the story in the first person, describes the funeral. Held by the "warm, smooth hand" of his father, he looks at "the dull, brown fingers" of the deceased, "tough like stumps of roots." "They will not dig any more in the field, they will not beat me. They wanted to tear back the new era. Time has cast them aside."

Three years after *Tinko*, Strittmatter published his novel *Der Wundertäter*. The former novel had been written with the Soviet cultural ideal in mind; the latter work, produced during the so-called "thaw" in East Germany, is far more liberal. The party literary arbiters had frowned on writers who were concerned principally with the past; now they relaxed in this regard. Many writers took advantage of the new freedom to describe the era with which they were more familiar. Thus, too, Strittmatter.

Der Wundertäter is the story of the first thirty years of Stanislaus Büdner, beginning in 1909. Stanislaus is a highly gifted child; he impresses the adults so much that they looked upon him as a miracle-worker. The matter-of-fact village police are less enthusiastic about him, however. Stanislaus leaves for a nearby town, where he becomes the apprentice of a baker who exploits him. His love for the pastor's daughter is frustrated because of the difference in social class standards. Stanislaus expresses his distress in verse. He gets along, however; he is dreamy, ingenuous, and cheerful, but also clever and crafty. There are many comic episodes in the book, the humor being often lusty and earthy. There are flirtations with gay maidens; buxom women are patted fondly on the bottom.

World War II breaks out, and the hero enters the army. There he meets many new people. He is especially impressed by Rolling, a manufacturer's son, a representative of the revolutionary workers and a poet. Stanislaus becomes more serious; he realizes the inhumanity of National Socialism. Rolling escapes and goes over to the Soviet army. Stanislaus deserts later and determines to fight for the revolution.

The somber East German critics had considerable difficulty in evaluating this gay book. In order to bring it into line with communist cultural ideals, they finally classified it as "a masterly socialistic novel of development."

The novel, however, is anything but socialistic. The milieu is definitely middle-class. The hero is not a serious-minded representative of the working class, but a happy, lusty knave who enjoys life. The satiric comments of Strittmatter do not refer to social or political conditions. The book was found to be very entertaining; it was widely read and even became a success in West Germany.

It was the third of his village novels, *Ole Bienkopp,* that established Strittmatter's fame. Published in 1963, it is a typical East German novel of the worker. He sets the tone of the book in the first five sentences.

The earth travels through space. Man sends forth iron pigeons and waits impatiently for their return. He waits for an olive branch from his brothers on the other stars. What is a village on this earth? It may be a spore on the skin of a decaying potato or a little red dot on the sunny side of a ripening apple.

Strittmatter then presents a colorful panorama of the everyday activities of the inhabitants of the village of Blumenau. Their joys and sorrows, their virtues and human failings, are described. There are discussions with party leaders about expanding the community and increasing production. The peasants are quite content; no longing is expressed for the good old times nor criticism of the new system.

Typical figures appear on the scene: the ambitious young party secretary, the fanatically loyal old maid, the pastor, the teacher, a dull-witted pietist, a humorless forester, an alcoholic, and a great many dull, simple-minded peasants. The villain is the capitalistically inclined Ramsch, the owner of the sawmill, who studied medicine for a short time in America and who spices his speech with bits of English, frequently incorrectly used.

Ole, the hero, is a headstrong and taciturn individual, who finally becomes the victim of his own stubborn nature. His pretty and sturdy wife, Angret, is seduced by Ramsch. He deserts her, and she takes her life in the lake where she and Ole romantically first made love. Ole also perishes in the reeds of the lake after working strenuously for several days in an effort to recover a piece of bad land for the community.

Strangely enough, the Soviet Union is hardly referred to— and then only as a somewhat foreign, distant concept. On the other hand the United States receives favorable mention. West Germany is completely ignored.

Strittmatter's style is simple, clear, and unadorned. He avoids regional or dialectic expressions. Descriptions of persons and objects are not detailed. His sentences are short, a paragraph usually consisting of only four or five. Strittmatter draws his characters with sharp lines, like woodcuts. He builds up situations with lively dialogue and much humor. Ole Bienkopp, because of his idealism and modesty, is a sympathetic character. He stands out from the narrow-minded peasants and the unimaginative party functionaries.

Although life in the village is hard, it is moving toward greater comfort and contentment. This thought Strittmatter expresses on the last page.

. . . a young woman climbs up the hill to the poultry farm. She is care-worn. Until now life has not showered her with roses. She opens a stall and a flock of ducks fly out. . . . She looks after the birds—a little bit of luck, a legacy. A smile hovers about her mouth, a shy little flame. . . .

Strittmatter is an optimist. He realizes that the East German critics are annoyed by his cheerful attitude toward life and his slighting of the political and ideological in his novels. At the conference of the League of Writers of East Germany in 1958 he said:

"To many of one's colleagues one is not acceptable if one looks too optimistically at our social development. What the devil—there must be something to criticize and satirize! . . . Since I am not a child of sadness,

I was at times impelled to banter and joke heartily . . . after all, I did not want to play the village fool. . . . What, however, made me completely sick was my proletarian optimism. That I couldn't hide for longer than an hour. . . . And, as far as my colleagues are concerned, I belong to the naive simplifiers, and I must say: I feel perfectly happy that way." [1]

The sincerity of this statement cannot be doubted. Strittmatter realizes he is no intellectual giant or genius. He is quite content to be an optimistic regional writer.

Stefan Heym (born 1913)

Stefan Heym is difficult to classify. Of German birth, he came to the United States in his youth and spent years here. He finally returned to East Germany but continues to write in English. Like the hero of his novel *The Crusaders* (1948), he does not seem to know where he belongs.

Heym was born in Chemnitz, Saxony on April 10, 1913. He was a student at the University of Berlin in 1933 when Hitler came into power. He was outspokenly anti-Nazi. At the age of eighteen he had published an antimilitary poem for which he was beaten up. Under sharp scrutiny because of his anti-Nazi views, he fled to Czechoslovakia, skiing part of the way across the mountains.

From 1933 to 1935 he lived in Prague, where he maintained himself by doing odd jobs and by writing. In 1935 he won a fellowship offered by the University of Chicago to graduate students whose studies had been interrupted by the Nazis. He came to the United States, obtained his M.A., and then became the editor of a small anti-Nazi paper in New York. The publication failed after two years, but in the meantime Heym had rendered a signal service in exposing the machinations of the local Nazi Bund. His findings were published in 1938 in a pamphlet entitled "Nazis in the U.S.A."

During his stay in the United States, Heym became interested in American literature. In 1937 his dramatized version of Mark Twain's *Tom Sawyer* was produced in Vienna and Prague.

The influence of American writers on him can be detected in *The Crusaders,* which reminds one of Mailer's *The Naked and the Dead.*

After the collapse of his anti-Nazi paper, Heym worked for three years as a printing salesman. In his free time he wrote his first novel, *Hostages* (1942), which describes the Nazi occupation of Prague in terms of the experiences of a group of hostages who are about to be shot. A German official had committed suicide; the Nazis accused the hostages of having caused his death. The book was given favorable comment; it was praised as an exciting story, although the characters are not too clearly drawn and the writing is somewhat uneven. It was, however, considered inferior to *Darkness at Noon* by Arthur Koestler, who had treated a similar theme. Orville Prescott, the critic of the *New York Times,* said it was an excellent portrayal of Nazis—"tense, tautly constructed, swift and terrible." The book sold widely and was made into a film.

In 1944 Heym published *Of Smiling Peace,* which was based on the war in Africa. He had entered the U.S. Army as a private in 1943 and had been sent to Europe. There he was promoted and became a lieutenant in the Division for Psychological Warfare. He took part in the American invasion of Normandy, the march through France, and the occupation of Germany. Then, because of his pro-communist leanings, he was discharged.

Heym returned to the United States and on the basis of his experiences on the continent published *The Crusaders* in English. The German edition, *Kreuzfahrer von heute* ("crusaders of today"), appeared in 1950. In this autobiographical novel Heym severely censures American occupation policies in Europe. With cynicism he describes the loose living of the conquerors.

His hero—with whom Heym may be identified—Sergeant Bing, enters Germany with mixed feelings. He is eager, for one thing, to see whether anything still binds him to the land of his forefathers. Having spent his childhood there, he feels he can determine rather definitely whether he has eliminated the German traits in him. He is surprised to find that he is not wholly American, that he has not completely rejected his Teutonic heritage. This dichotomy causes his ruin.

Heym, who was in a similar dilemma, later sent his officer's credentials and war decorations back to the President and settled in East Germany (1953).

The Crusaders, like Heym's first novel, received favorable reviews. One critic wrote: "The novel has everything—combat, pursuit, cruelty, sex, a host of characters . . . and a story that plunges ahead like an armored division. It also has a thesis and a sound one, namely, that the war was fought against evils, some of which exist in our own army and nation. There is only one thing the novel lacks: the respect for his characters and for truth as opposed to bombast. . . ."

In 1951 Heym published *The Eyes of Reason.* This novel is about Czechoslovakia being taken over by the communists. Heym slants his story deliberately in favor of the new regime. In 1953 he published *Goldsborough,* a novel which has as its background the strike in an American mine.

Heym was grateful for the asylum given him by America during the Hitler regime, but he found a complete lack of understanding here of his idealism in fighting, as a soldier and as a writer, to free Germany from the Nazis. He was disappointed in the American character. In *The Crusaders* he makes many cynical comments, such as the following:

Yasha could not help being amazed at the American. What ability to blend concern for the welfare of mankind with sound business practice! The Germans were orphans compared to it; they had covered their unashamed bullying and grabbing with love for the Fatherland—lately, they had dropped even that pretense. But the Americans really believed their own liberalism. At least this Major did. A healthy people. They had achieved the perfect amalgam of God, democracy, and the interest rate. Too bad that they were running up against the unashamed decadence of Europe.

Is Heym an American or a German writer? He is claimed on both sides, although the East German critics would be happy to drop him entirely and leave him to the Americans. He is not included in the comprehensive *Deutsche Literaturgeschichte.*

Stephan Hermlin *(born 1915)*

In 1915 Rudolf Leder was born in Chemnitz, Saxony. In his youth he was a printer's apprentice. An active communist, he emigrated in 1936. After wandering through Egypt, Palestine, England, and France, he reached Switzerland, where he was interned.

In 1945 in Zurich, under the pseudonym of Stephan Hermlin, his first literary production appeared. It was a collection of poems entitled *Zwölf Balladen von den großen Städten* ("twelve ballads of the big cities").

The ballads in this first volume are rich in symbolism and imagery. They maintain a lofty and majestic dignity throughout, reminiscent of Stephan Mallarmé. Evidently the young German author, in admiration of the French poet whom he imitated, assumed the latter's given name. And the fine-sounding Hermlin, suggestive of ermine and quite in consonance with the elegance of his verse, replaced the very ordinary Leder ("leather").

The name is far more than a mere *nom de plume;* it is indicative of the poet's innermost feelings and temperament. Although a faithful communist, Hermlin is basically an esthete. His wide reading has made him sensitive to many poetic styles— baroque, neoromantic, expressionistic, and surrealist. In addition to Mallarmé, he has been strongly influenced by other French poets, particularly Rimbaud. His translations from the Spanish, Turkish, Hungarian, and American Negro lyrics are skillfully done.

Hermlin's verse is formal, stately, elegant, and festive. He prefers French and Italian measures. His imagery scintillates with references to splendid palaces, lofty cathedrals, marble fountains, and graceful swans. Tolling bells and every type of musical instrument are brought in for sound effects. He leans to preciosity. In a poem, "Die toten Städte" ("the dead cities"), he writes:

Suns, whither is gone
Your resounding wheel?
Embraced by beauty

> Apollonian sowing,
> Flutes and marble forms,
> Stars in the evening tree,
> Smiling maidens, thou mild one,
> Whither did you pass away, dream?

One would never suspect the writer of these lines to be a communist. There is a complete absence of revolutionary fervor. future. Loneliness, fatigue, resignation, and longing for death In fact, there is not the slightest tone of optimism, of belief in the predominate. The words "night," "death," and "black" occur in almost every one of Hermlin's poems.

That a poet of such tendencies should get into difficulties with the communist literary critics is not surprising. Hermlin realized the disparity; he tried valiantly to overcome it. As a loyal communist he made strenuous efforts to adjust his verse to the demands of the party.

In 1940 he wrote "Ballade von den weitschauenden Augen" ("ballad of the far-seeing eyes"), in which he sings of the "ruby-studded towers of the Kremlin" and praised the two hundred millions who "are sowing the seed of tomorrow's world."

In 1945 he tried even harder to conform. He realized that to reach the masses he would have to change his style and his language. This thought he expresses in "Ballade von den alten und den neuen Worten" ("ballad of the old and new words"). He rejects his former language regretfully, however:

> I suffer because of my words!
> And the words were beautiful. . . .

He begs for a new language:

> Therefore, give me a language,
> I am surrendering mine to you.

He is aware of the urgent need for a new medium:

> I want a new language,
> Like someone who chooses his tool.

His efforts did not meet with success; he could not entirely discard his characteristic language. Even in the ballads written after 1945, death and bitterness sometimes reappear. In a ballad, "Hope," he writes:

> Forbidden spring, toward which we bore,
> By the oppressed you are called hope.

Hermlin's older verse was of little interest or importance to the East German critics; in fact, some of it was suspect. It is significant that the *Zweiundzwanzig Balladen* ("twenty-two ballads"), which appeared in 1947 in East Berlin, received a West German literary award.

When Hermlin appealed for "a new language," he was referred to Johannes R. Becher, the model German communist poet. Hermlin had little regard, however, for Becher's art. He called it "conventional versifying." Actually, he faced the same dilemma that Becher did when he came to East Germany; that is, to develop a clear, simple mode of expression, intelligible to the masses.

Hermlin's most valiant effort resulted in the volume of poems entitled *Der Flug der Taube* (1952; "the flight of the dove"). In it he deliberately eliminated all the metaphorical extravagances and classical allusions of his earlier ballads. Attempting to imitate Soviet verse, he chose revolutionary themes. He extolled the October Revolution of 1917 and the defense of Stalingrad; he praised Stalin and Wilhelm Pieck, the first president of East Germany.

Hermlin found it difficult, however, to completely drop his former symbols. To one of these, the night, he gave a new meaning. Night represents the good, the desirable, the ideal. In the poem "Aurora" in the collection *Der Flug der Taube*, he rhapsodizes:

> For the sake of this one night all music was written,
> For the sake of this one night every new thought was
>   thought,
> Every heart had its home in the world,
> Every abandoned one could love.
> Whatever happened, happened for this night.

From these idealistic lyrical heights Hermlin drops suddenly to pour panegyrics over Stalin.

Then descended from the mountain
The summoner, the teacher.
Out of the portals of the clefts
He came forth, the man of Gori.
He raised the curtain of the mists.
Across his forehead
The rainbow of the waterfall shone.

Despite all efforts, however, to adjust to the East German literary climate, Hermlin was deeply dissatisfied and quite unhappy. This is evident in the poem "Forderung des Tages" ("challenge of the day").

Tell, language of the poet, tarter than elderberry,
Voice of the day, flute of the night, endless flight
Of unriddled birds, marvelous miracle,
Tell the cry and the silence, the thirst and the jug.

That blinded I gaze, that in the stream of toccatas
Deafened I waste away, in the shadow of the script,
You do that. Nevermore may I dispense with you,
Until at the shadowed tower the lance strikes me.

I waste away, waste away . . . That you never get over it,
That you call me a thorn in your flesh,
That for evermore remorse and guilt cling to you,
That the suffering of the most distant peoples burns in you.

I hear the sweet violins of what is to come.
The oboes of the dead bewitch my blood.
White cities! You swans of the future! You roundelay
Of those murdered, take me into your care!

Hermlin did not find it possible to achieve the synthesis toward which he strove. He tried to be a subtle lyricist and a revolutionary agitator; he wanted to be a West European esthete and an East German popular poet. It did not suit his temperament at all. As a gentle, sensitive soul, he found it impossible to scream forth propaganda. Curiously enough, his development was the same as that of Becher, whom he had derided earlier; his art, too, turned into "neoclassic suavity and conventional versifying." *Der Flug der Taube* showed that he had landed in a blind alley.

Hermlin is predominantly a poet. He has, however, also written very creditable prose. His style is refined and cultured. He gives evidence of having studied Thomas Mann, Kafka, Hemingway, Sartre, and Camus. His language, his plots, and the atmosphere he creates, as well as the characters he portrays, are the work of a skilled craftsman. He builds up dramatic episodes in prisons and concentration camps. The only weakness is that his novels lack warmth; they do not grip the reader. He is, however, regarded in East Germany as one of the most gifted novelists.

His first story, "Der Leutnant Yorck von Wartenburg" (1946; Lieutenant Yorck of Wartenburg), seeks to establish an ideological connection between the unsuccessful attempt of July 20, 1944, to assassinate Hitler and the vaunted idealism of the Soviets. This is done in a unique manner. Lieutenant Yorck, condemned to death for his part in the affair, dreams during the last moments of his life that he has escaped and fled to Russia, "that great land in which everything was fully understood: honor, fidelity, duty, and home."

Even in his prose narrative Hermlin's poetic nature breaks through. There are lyrical passages. What gives the story charm and interest is the psychological skill with which he depicts the hallucinations of the officer, rather than the projection of political ideas.

Hermlin's second short story, "Reise eines Malers in Paris" (1947; "journey of a painter in Paris"), is also based on dreams and hallucinations. The surrealist devices employed to create an atmosphere of illusion, fear, and vagueness are reminiscent of Kafka. The leading character is a German emigré, a painter, who finds himself confronted by all kinds of mysterious and inexplicable powers in Paris. During his absence, many strangers have penetrated his room. He tries to tell himself that he is not afraid, but then the thought occurs that the strangers might attack him and throw him out of the window.

On an imaginary journey he arrives in Barcelona during the Spanish Civil War. He sees "a related, entirely unknown universe" in the "impotence of a nightmare." The painter's second stop is in a town in France, where he is interned. The camp is situated in a ghostly, mysterious landscape, where the prisoner is pursued by "the soft sliding and whispering of swooning shadows" and where, "like a drowning person, he felt water flowing between his eyelids." In a third vision he lands in Red China, where he gets a cordial reception but can find no release. The words "nightmare," "menace," "impotence," and "exhaustion" occur repeatedly.

Neither the form nor the content of these stories pleased the East German critics. They accused Hermlin of employing the dacadent surrealistic style and of portraying merely passive heroes. In an effort to satisfy the critics, Hermlin produced a collection of short stories entitled *Die Zeit der Gemeinsamkeit* (1949; "the time of common interest").

One of the best stories is "Die Zeit der Einsamkeit" ("the time of loneliness"). A German emigré has fled with his wife to Paris. Again there are some surrealist visions, but action on the part of the protagonist is introduced at the end. Neubert, depressed and unhappy, sees the fear and loneliness in the eyes of his wife, Magda. A Frenchman, a Pétain adherent, rapes her. She dies. Neubert is roused to action and kills the criminal. Then the political angle is introduced. Sought by the police, the hero determines to join the communists and fight against the Pétain regime.

This sort of practical application is introduced, somewhat awkwardly, in a number of Hermlin's tales. In the short story "Der Weg der Bolschewiki" ("the way of the Bolsheviks") the narrative, which at times is quite moving, is spoiled by an overdose of propaganda. The officer, who tells the story in the first person in the form of notes, letters, and diary entries, finds time during the holocaust to comment leisurely on life, literature, and art. Hermlin's poetic nature cannot be restrained even while he is writing what could be purely narrative or documentary prose. Incidentally, Hermlin has no scruples about distorting facts; he makes good use of poetic license. And he constantly introduces poetical expressions and metaphors that do not fit in with the character of the narrative.

In "Der Weg der Bolschewiki" Hermlin goes to extremes in his efforts to present communist ideology. A dying Soviet officer, who is being tortured in a German concentration camp, apparently has no other worry but to ask himself why he did not join the Communist Party. A fellow prisoner reassures him that, if he survives, he will make out the required application for the distressed officer. The startling idea suggested here by Hermlin is that even a dead man can be accepted as a member of the party. Another prisoner, an equally dedicated German communist, plans to give a secret course on the development of communism to his fellow prisoners.

Evidently, even the East German critics felt that some of these incidents were far-fetched. Hermlin's reputation declined. For several years he wrote only essays and magazine articles. In 1951 he published a volume entitled *Erste Reihe* ("first series"), a collection of rather well-drawn portraits of German underground resistance fighters, intended for young readers.

Then, in 1954, he published in a magazine a story, "Die Kommandeuse" ("the commandant"), which aroused much discussion, perturbation, and unfavorable comment. It portrays a former, woman SS-commander (*Kommandeuse*), Erna Dorn, who is serving a term of fifteen years in a prison camp at Halle, East Germany, for her crimes against humanity. During the uprising in Berlin on June 17, 1953—now commemorated as a national holiday in West Germany—she is freed and acclaimed the heroic representative of the political prisoners. The startling implication made by Hermlin is that not dissatisfied workers but former Nazis engineered the uprising. Erna Dorn is arrested, almost immediately, and condemned to death.

The story outraged West German as well as East German critics. The latter asserted that the sympathetic analysis of her psychological reactions by Hermlin aroused pity for her. The fact is that Hermlin did make her portrait far more vivid than that of many a communist hero whom he has depicted. The style, too, annoyed the party functionaries; Hermlin, they said, had returned to his earlier surrealism. And why so much detail on the inner life of a vicious woman Nazi and little or nothing on the heroism of the workers?

"Die Kommandeuse" was rejected with such vehemence that it practically finished Hermlin's literary career. All he did after that was to collect his poems in two volumes, *Dichtungen* (1956; "poems") and *Nachdichtungen* (1957; "paraphrases"), and to write occasional essays and magazine articles. In these he has attempted to defend his point of view. He was ready to make a compromise between art and propaganda, but it was evident that he was not ready to surrender completely.

Because of his friendly assistance to a number of young and liberal-minded poets, he was censured and relieved of his job as secretary of the German Academy of Arts. His groveling acceptance of his discharge is pathetic. His public statement contained the following:

> This decision was just and I, like the other members, approve it. I was not the right man in the right place. . . . I committed a series of mistakes. Often I have viewed poetry and art, which have almost filled my life, as independent of the time and place in which they expressed themselves. I acknowledge this as a mistake, but I also know that I am not entirely immune to a repetition of this mistake.

The confession closes with the customary assurance of unswerving loyalty. Hermlin, as an artist, has been silenced.

Johannes Bobrowski (born 1917)

Johannes Bobrowski, who is a gifted poet as well as an accomplished novelist, was born in 1917 in Tilsit, the former capital of Prussian Lithuania. His father was a railroad worker. As a young man Bobrowski studied the history of art in Berlin. He was a soldier in World War II and was taken prisoner. Upon his release he returned to the great plain east of the Oder.

With his vivid descriptions and colorful characterizations of the population, Bobrowski has introduced his native region to East German literature. He does this especially in his best book, which bears the peculiar title *Levins Mühle: 34 Sätze über meinen Großvater* ("Levin's mill: 34 sentences about my grandfather"). It appeared in 1964, simultaneously in both East and

West Germany—something very unusual. The subject matter reminds one of Günter Grass; the style resembles that of Uwe Johnson and Peter Weiss.

The historic background and the locale of the novel are somewhat unusual, even for the better informed German reader. Bobrowski describes life in a West Prussian village on the Polish border in the year 1874. It is the time of the *"Kulturkampf"* and the campaign of Germanization, conducted amid a medley of Poles, Germans, Jews, gypsies, Catholics, Baptists, Methodists, Adventists, and Mennonites. There are ironic digs at the allegedly superior and "pious" Germans. Many of them have Polish names, whereas many of the Poles have German names.

The plot is a simple one. The author's grandfather, a rich miller, wishing to get rid of an unwelcome Jewish rival, Levin, has the latter's mill swept down the stream by opening the sluices. The case is brought to court. After much wrangling, an effort is made to rescue justice. At the close of the book the author hands the case over to a painter, who is to transform the question of guilt into a painting.

One of the basic ideas of the novel is that the misdeeds of the grandparents are passed down to later generations. This idea is expressed at the beginning of Chapter 9 in the following words:

> The fifteenth sentence does not belong to the action.
> Even if [it refers] to us, it runs not quite exactly:
> The sins of the fathers are visited on the children
> Into the third and fourth generation.

Though the plot is simple enough, the action does not proceed smoothly at all. In fact, the author often loses the thread of the plot and occasionally digresses to tell anecdotes or introduce extraneous ideas. The main action is almost lost in the tangle of humorous comments, colorful descriptions, and little stories.

The handling of the "34 sentences" is unique. Bobrowski introduces the first one right at the beginning. It is: "The Drewenz is a tributary in Poland." He discusses this statement briefly and concludes, ". . . that's no good as a beginning. So, then, a new first sentence."

The author follows this style throughout the book, addressing the reader, taking him into his confidence, and trying to come to an understanding with him. There is a constant mingling of leisurely narrative and factual report. Rather amusing are the five dreams of the grandfather, which are dispersed throughout the book. Each one is entitled *"Geistererscheinung"* (apparition).

Bobrowski ends his novel as follows:

The story could have happened in so many places and in so many different regions; it was only to be related here. In thirty-four sentences. Four sentences, then, are still missing. Here they are:

Come, let's sing.

In Gollub the gypsies are playing.

If we don't sing, others will sing.

Now only a single sentence is missing. At that moment Philippi the painter jumps with a little hop over the curb and stands there with outspread arms: Well, must I still explain something to you?

Then my grandfather says: I don't think so. And goes back a step. And says with a rather insecure look: Do leave me in peace.

No, cries the painter Philippi, turns like a top on his heel and claps his hands close to my grandfather's nose. As if he had caught a fly. And this Philippian No, that goes. For us it counts here as a last sentence.

Johannes Bobrowski is one of the few East German authors whose works are published and widely read in West Germany.

Franz Fühmann   *(born 1922)*

Franz Fühmann is considered one of the outstanding poets of East Germany, but he is also a talented writer of prose. His distinguishing character trait is unswerving loyalty to communist ideology and to East Germany.

He was born in 1922 in a small Bohemian town, the son of an apothecary. In his boyhood he idolized Hitler; with pride he donned the brown uniform, and in 1939 he volunteered for the German army. He served on several fronts, including those in Russia and Greece. After being taken a prisoner, he spent four years in a Soviet prison camp. There, in the fall of 1947, he was invited to attend lecture courses in communism.

The clarity and the logic of the theories that were presented to him fascinated him. Within a short time he was fully convinced of the truth of Marxism. He was eager to serve the revolution. The former SA-man had turned into an ardent communist.

In December of 1949 he was discharged and went to East Germany. He had published his first poems in 1942 in Hamburg. Now he resumed his writing; his verse was published in *Aufbau*, the leading East German literary monthly.

His first collection of poems was entitled *Die Nelke Nikos* (1953; "the carnation of Nikos"). In these poems Fühmann expresses his deep hatred of National Socialism, his adherence to the ideals of the Soviet Union, and his patriotic dedication to East Germany. He produced exactly the sort of verse that was expected of him. In this he was absolutely sincere; he espoused the new gospel with the fervor of a neophyte. The object of his adulation was new, but the style of his poems was that of his former Nazi lyrics.

> Take our hands, Germany, Fatherland, take the
> Glowing heart full of love and hate, take the
> Voice of the intractable will: Yes, we
> Come to work, to fight, to bear you
> Germany, land of our love, through the ripening of time.
> . . . And we bring you, holy, other Germany,
> Our lives as the stones to build your future.

In fact, not only Fühmann's style but his ideas were those of his Nazi past. He manifests the greatest eagerness to get into line, to obey, and to follow.

> Let's sing songs of battle and victory:
> We're building the Germany of tomorrow!

He transferred his ardent devotion from National Socialism to communism, trustfully accepting everything, ready to do the bidding of his superiors. Fühmann promotes the propaganda of East Germany with the utmost zeal and fidelity. Nowhere in his works can the slightest note of dissatisfaction or criticism be found. Even when the so-called "thaw"—the period of relaxed censorship—set in in 1956, Fühmann brusquely rejected the greater freedom of expression allowed the writers. In his poem "Narrenfreiheit" ("fools' freedom") he censured those who wanted more liberty.

> Today there are very independent
> Spirits in fools' garb.
> They strive to get out of the narrowness
> Of the everyday and the fatherland.
> High in the sky, in the satin of the cloud,
> They see the home of freedom . . .
> They consider themselves the descendants
> Of court fools, when for their art
> They cry loudly for freedom, which allows
> Them, in fitful fancies
> To disavow thinking and serving,
> To flee from the demands of the time.

In 1961 many of the leading authors, among them Anna Seghers, Willi Bredel, Bodo Uhse, Eduard Claudius, and Stephan Hermlin, declined to picture East German conditions in glowing colors and treated other themes. Fühmann, however, in that year published an enthusiastic report on the shipbuilding docks in Rostock, *Kabelkran und blauer Peter* ("cable-crane and blue Peter"). A second book of his, written in the same year, *Spuk* ("spook"), gave a rosy picture of the "heroic" everyday activities of the people's police (*Volkspolizei*).

Fühmann does possess ability. Even though the longer poem "Die Fahrt nach Stalingrad" ("the journey to Stalingrad") contains some unbearable banalities, there are passages that demonstrate the skill of the poet in dealing with his past. A young German has a revelation while he is in Russia and discovers his true fatherland. German imperialism and militarism are denounced, and the brighter future under socialism is presented. One of his favorite themes is the emergence of the disillusioned man out of National Socialism and World War II.

The East German literary arbiters did not favor the idea of devoting so much attention to the past; the writers who did so

were suspected of evading contemporary problems. Hence, Fühmann stopped writing about the past.

Fühmann established his reputation as a poet through his
collection entitled *Aber die Schöpfung soll dauern* (1957; "but
creation is to last"). It radiates the optimistic faith of East
German ideologists in the creative power of man. An example of
this ideal are the following stanzas from the poem "Die Kinder
am Strand" ("the children at the beach"):

> But creation must endure!
> The miraculous happens:
> After the fright, the mourning,
> The hand again becomes active,
> And it compels the difficult hours,
> So that the castle, the mountain, arise,
> And, again overcome,
> It overcomes again the sea,
> And deep in the soul within
> Something is already conscious:
> Thou canst no longer escape it,
> The sweet, demanding joy,
> To build hills and castles,
> With bridges and towers and gate,
> So as no longer with horror to look at
> The surge of the sea.

Many of the younger East German writers had served in the
army of the Third Reich and had even been members of the
National Socialist Party. In an effort to slough off their undem-
ocratic past and to prove that they were "good Germans," they
wrote books that denounced the imperialist war and the horrors
of Nazism.

In 1955 Fühmann published a novella entitled *Kameraden*
("comrades"), which was filmed under the title *Betrogen bis zum
jüngsten Tag* ("cheated until the day of judgment"). It reveals
the viciousness of the comradeship of the Nazi soldiers, who were
brothers in arms in the pursuit of inhumanity.

Fühmann continued to write novelle and short stories. A collection of the latter is entitled *Das Judenauto* (1962; "the Jew's

auto"). The best of his poems were published in the collection *Die Richtung der Märchen* (1962; "the direction of the fairytales").

Fühmann's books and films have met with a favorable reception. Equally successful has been his collection of stories *Stürzende Schatten* ("falling shadows"), published in 1958. Fühmann has also done several children's books, among them a revision of Goethe's *Reineke Fuchs* (1966).

For his many contributions to East German literature, Fühmann has been given five national literary awards at various times.

Dieter Noll   (born 1927)

Dieter Noll, the son of an apothecary, was born in 1927 in Riesa, Saxony. Like most of the other socialist authors of his age group he was drafted into the German army. Captured in action, he was put into an American prison camp.

After his return he made his first contacts with the working-class movement. In 1946 he joined the Communist Party. At the University of Jena he studied German literature, the history of art, and philosophy. In 1950 he was made an editor of *Aufbau*, the literary magazine in East Berlin.

After writing some short stories, Noll published his first book, *Die Dame Perlon* (1953; "lady Perlon"), which treats various problems in the building up of the socialist state.

Like a number of other socialist authors returning from the war, he found it difficult to get back into civilian life. He wrote his major work on the basis of his experiences in the war.

This novel, *Die Abenteuer des Werner Holt* (1960; "the adventures of Werner Holt"), tells the story of the political development of a young man (Noll himself) during his service in the army. Werner Holt at first is very friendly with his fellow soldiers Wolzow and Gomulka; gradually the disparity among the three widens. Wolzow, the son of an army officer, is a typical militarist, daring and brilliant. He loses his life in action. Holt admires his courage and self-assurance; later he hates and despises him.

Holt, accepting the officially stated aims of the war, cannot believe that the rumors of the Nazi atrocities are true. He is gradually enlightened by the talkative wife of an SS-man and by Gomulka, who works hard to convince Holt. Even at the close of the novel Holt is still a little skeptical.

The second part of the book appeared in 1963; it was titled *Roman einer Heimkehr* ("novel of a return home"). Noll set out to describe the further development of the character of his hero in civilian life. Holt has lengthy discussions with his fiancée, Gundel, whose ideological attitude disturbs him. As the son of academically trained parents, he is inclined to reject middle-class standards. For a time he sways mentally between East and West Germany, like a wanderer between two worlds. The prosperity of West Germany, its "economic miracle," is repulsive to him. Holt returns to East Germany to continue his studies.

The East German critics were sorely disappointed in this solution; they expected the hero to embark on an active political career. Noll has promised to present the final social and political reorientation of his hero in a third volume.

Noll has received three awards in literature, including the National Prize.

Christa Wolf   (born 1929)

In general the party exercises a rather severe control over what is published. Unfavorable comments on social and economic conditions are permitted, but no criticism of party leadership or the communist system is tolerated. Occasionally, however, a book appears that is unusually critical, which affords proof to the more liberal-minded that not all criticism of prevailing conditions has been suppressed. As an example of this the novel *Der geteilte Himmel* (1963; The Divided Sky) by Christa Wolf may be cited.

Christa Wolf, the daughter of a merchant, was born in 1929 in Landsberg, Bavaria. She worked for a time as the secretary of the mayor of a small village in Mecklenburg. Then she studied German literature at the University of Jena. As a young author she rose rapidly, becoming the editor of the journal *Neue deutsche Literatur.* Much of what she has written is based on personal experiences.

Christa Wolf is especially gifted in portraying women. This is evident in her first book, *Moskauer Novelle* (1961). A German woman doctor, Vera, is friendly with Pawel, an officer in the Russian army. He had entered her village at the end of the war. Their relationship is warm, but they part. Fifteen years later Vera meets Pawel again, while visiting Moscow. It seems as if their love were about to be rekindled. Both, however, have married, have children, and have changed. Is their relationship of 1945 to be resumed? Christa Wolf's motivation is psychologically sound, especially with reference to Vera. The latter's heroic self-denial is the result of her feminine way of thinking and feeling.

The same motif appears in Christa Wolf's second and most successful book, *Der geteilte Himmel.* It was published the following year, in 1964, in West Germany, an unusual accomplishment. This novel is far superior to her first one in plot, language, and literary devices. In fact, since Uwe Johnson's *Mutmaßungen über Jakob* has never been published in East Germany, it may be considered the first notable East German novel about partitioned Germany.

Christa Wolf and Johnson develop their stories through extensive flashback. In both novels the explanation of the accident happening to the leading character is deliberately left vague. On the other hand, whereas Johnson ruminates, investigates, and repeats himself without coming to a definite solution, Christa Wolf has her heroine Rita decide unequivocally against following her lover to West Germany.

Rita's lover, Manfred, a young engineer, is a rather unattractive type. He is cynical, mocking, and discourteous. Despite these unpleasant qualities, Rita loves him. In fact, she even moves into his home and eats her evening meals in the company of the unstable father, whom Manfred hates, and the cold mother, whom Manfred despises. Rita, who is preparing to be a teacher, ideally motivated enters a "workers' brigade" in a railroad coach factory, where she is injured in an accident. Her story is told from her memories on her hospital bed.

It is almost clear from the beginning that the two lovers are not suited to one another. The cool, intelligent young Manfred looks upon political sentiment as something absurd. He is practical-minded; he wants a good job and a comfortable life. His eyes turn to West Berlin, which he visits with Rita. At that time it was still possible to pass from East Berlin to West Berlin on the U-Bahn.

Manfred urges Rita to flee with him. She, however, is staunchly loyal to East Germany. Younger and less experienced than he, she was happy to leave the village in her youth and study at the university. She is optimistic about the future of East Germany.

She tries to visualize life with Manfred in West Berlin, but it seems foreign and repulsive to her. Even the fact that the same language is spoken makes no difference. Rita's attitude is intended to reflect the fact that a national feeling has developed among the younger generation in East Germany. The glamor of West Berlin does not lure her; she remains true to her community, even at the cost of losing Manfred. He leaves her and goes to West Berlin.

Despite the fact that she lets her heroine express such implicit loyalty to the socialist state, Christa Wolf does not present a very attractive picture of social and political conditions in East Germany. She castigates the excesses of party politics unmercifully. Several of the professional communists she portrays are among the most repulsive characters appearing in any East German novel. Nevertheless, in 1963, Christa Wolf, like her Rita, believed firmly in the future of communism. The unpleasant features and the instances of mismanagement and social injustice were, presumably, transitional phenomena that would be over-

This faith, however, is not expressed in Christa Wolf's latest come in time.

book, *Nachdenken über Christa T.* (1967; Thinking about Christa T.). Quite the contrary: a profound distrust of the atmosphere prevailing in East Germany is revealed. A decidedly negative picture is given of the communist state with its bombastic speeches, its noisy parades, and the subservience of the average man to those in authority.

This well-written novel consists of a psychological biography of Christa T., a former schoolmate of Christa Wolf. Christa T.'s career and her thinking are portrayed on the basis of diaries, letters, and unfinished essays. Although she is intelligent and fearless, this schoolteacher, a university graduate married to a veterinarian, is not depicted as a heroine. She lives peacefully with her provincial husband, has three children in a house on the Baltic, and dies of leukemia at the age of thirty-five.

The pith of the characterization of Christa T. is in her rich *vie intérieure*. Her disgust with the readiness of her pupils to repeat propaganda slogans and her constant search for the development of a free, vital personality reveal a courageous and independent individual. The opinions she expresses are a far cry from those usually found in socialist literature. It is no wonder that the censors held up the publication of the book for two years. They finally permitted it to be printed in a limited edition of 400 copies and restricted its sale to professionally engaged adults. At the Sixth East German Writers Congress in the spring of 1969, the book was severely attacked by some critics but highly praised by others. This controversial novel, which is the best that has been produced recently in East Germany, will undoubtedly be printed in West Germany.

Karl Heinz Jakobs   *(born 1929)*

Karl Heinz Jakobs, born in East Prussia in 1929, quite clearly shows the influence of English and American writers in his novels and stories. He breaks with the tradition of the *neue Sachlichkeit* and develops his own style in describing life, as he sees it, in East Germany. In his major work, *Beschreibung eines Sommers* (1961; "description of a summer"), he presents a convincing love story set in a vast construction site at a mineral oil center.

When Tom and Grit meet for the first time, he gives her a crushing handshake. The conversation reminds one of Hemingway.

> "Ouch," she cried, "man, can't you watch out a little!"
> She felt her right shoulder and made a grimace. Her eyes sparkled.

There wasn't the least bit of embarrassment between us.
   "Did it hurt very much?" I asked with ironic sympathy.
   "Terrible," she said. "Were you a prizefighter once?"
   "Yes, yes," I said. "It's tough for someone who's so strong."
   "How strong are you?"
   "Here, please feel my muscles."

Tom, a young engineer, is a Don Juan but a good worker whom the woman director of the work cadre has sent to a larger construction job partly as a disciplinary measure. She recognizes his ability but adds, "Morally you're dirt." Having lately returned from the war, Tom is quite cynical. Suddenly, however, a bright, new day dawns for him: he falls in love with the attractive young woman machinist Grit. Unfortunately, she is already married; in fact, her husband is a communist functionary. The affection between Tom and Grit grows steadily; Tom's character and outlook begin to change. Finally the party reaches into the illicit romance. Tom is transferred to Berlin, and Grit is dropped from the party. The love story is well motivated; the attitudes and actions of the communists likewise.

Herbert Nachbar   (born 1930)

Herbert Nachbar, the son of a fisherman, set out to study medicine in Berlin in 1950. He gave this up, however, and became a reporter and editor instead. In his spare time he began his first novel, *Der Mond hat einen Hof* (1956; "The moon has a halo"), which is set in a village at the time of Kaiser Wilhelm II. What distinguishes this first work of the young author from so many other regional novels is the fact that he deliberately avoids the introduction of ideological material. Nachbar devotes his skill to the delineation of character and to the presentation of a colorful background.
   Der Tod des Admirals (1960; "the death of the admiral") was followed by his major work, the novel *Die Hochzeit von Länneken* (1960; "the wedding of Länneken"). Nachbar sets his Romeo-Juliet story in a Baltic fishing village where new social conditions have developed due to the organization of a fisher-

man's socialistic cooperative. The two lovers, Henning and Babs, struggle to achieve their marriage in the face of the deeply rooted traditions of property and social station of the old-fashioned parents. The wedding ends the long enmity between the two wealthiest families of the village and is the symbol of a new social and political order. The fishing grounds are made communal property. The fathers, "the admiral" and "the king" accept, not too gracefully, the collectivization of their former possessions. The two reactionaries are the best-drawn characters in the novel.

Since the milieu of the fishing village is thoroughly familiar to Nachbar from his childhood, his descriptions of the waterfront are accurate and colorful. To add to the verisimilitude of his dialogue, he occasionally uses the Low German regional dialect of the natives; but he does not use it so extensively that the reader familiar only with High German cannot still follow without difficulty.

Nachbar's *Die Hochzeit von Länneken* and the novel *Oben fährt der große Wagen* (1963: "up above the big wagon goes by") were made into motion pictures.

Equally successful has been Nachbar's novel *Haus unterm Regen* (1965; "house under rain"). In it he presents the personal problems of an East German military pilot whose fiancée is the daughter of an incorrigible Nazi living in West Germany.

Erik Neutsch   (born 1931)

Erik Neutsch was born in Schönebeck, Anhalt, in 1931, the son of an iron-moulder. He was considered the head of the workers' literary movement (*Arbeiterdichtung*) after the First Bitterfeld Conference of 1959. He was so impressed by this gathering that upon his return home he dashed off "Regengeschichte" (1960; "story of rain"). Its theme is the tension between the intelligentsia and the proletariat, which breaks out on the occasion of an accident in an industrial plant.

Neutsch included this story in a collection, *Bitterfelder Geschichten* ("Bitterfeld stories"), which he published in 1961. In 1964 his major work appeared, namely, *Spur der Steine* ("trail of stones"). It falls into the category of the novel of development (*Erziehungsroman*) with a number of stereotypes that occur regularly in East German narratives. It is obvious from the start that the hard-working, crude, girl-watching Balla will grow ideologically. One day he meets Katrin Klee, the pretty young engineer, who is expecting a child. The father of the child is Werner Horrath, the married party secretary. The members of the party are pictured as severe, unrelenting, and arbitrary. Horrath goes to ruin as a stone-breaker after being discharged. Balla's father, a loyal communist, dies in desperation because of the mismanagement of some of the party functionaries. Katrin flees after an embarrassing and painful cross-examination.

Neutsch's aim is to picture the development of a more human communism. Joy is to be found in one's work. Balla is to be happy setting stones. Slowly but steadily his qualities of leadership are brought out. He and the younger forces are to take over the torpid apparatus of the older generation. The wild, undisciplined Balla has been tamed; he becomes part of the socialist collective. As a member of the Communist Party he journeys about, introducing new and more efficient methods of production.

Brigitte Reimann   (born 1933)

Brigitte Reimann, a schoolteacher from Magdeburg, wrote her first book at the age of twenty-three. This book, *Die Frau am Pranger* (1956; "the woman at the pillory"), became very popular. It was written in dime-novel style and told the story of the love affair between a young German peasant girl, Kathrin, and a Russian prisoner of war. Next Brigitte Reimann published *Kinder von Hellas* ("children of Hellas"), which is based on the communist guerilla activity of 1948–50 in Greece.

Then, in consonance with the recommendations of the Bitterfeld Conference, the author "went into production." She entered the soft-coal works, Schwarze Pumpe, at Hoyerswerda, to see for herself what takes place in industry. Together with her husband, Siegfried Pitschmann, she wrote some radio plays and several shorter works that were not a success.

She displays her ability better in the story "Die Geschwister" (1963; "brother and sister"), which treats the same theme as Christa Wolf's *Der geteilte Himmel*. The action is confined to two days of 1961. Elisabeth and her fiancé, Joachim, try to dissuade her brother Uli, a young marine engineer, from flight to West Germany. The story consists of the description of four mental excursions into the past, which are held together loosely.

Since a brother is involved, the tension between lovers pictured by Christa Wolf is absent. The conflict, however, is sharper and more inexorable. A younger brother, Konrad, had fled earlier. Elisabeth's words, "I don't want to go through this again—of having a brother go away from my family, my republic," are significant. The idea of national consciousness and loyalty is stressed.

Uwe Johnson (born 1934)

Most of the older East German writers began to write before the division of Germany, and their earlier works describe conditions in the Reich. It is also true, however, that there are writers who began in East Germany and went to West Germany.

Uwe Johnson was born in 1934 in Pomerania and grew up in East Germany. He attended school in a little town in Mecklenburg. Later, he studied German literature at the universities of Rostock and Leipzig. Until 1959 he was a citizen of East Germany.

His first literary effort was a novel, *Ingrid Babendererde*. Rejected by Aufbau, the leading East German publishing house, it was never published. In fact, none of Johnson's writings has been published in the East; it is quite obvious that they will have none of him. He is not even mentioned in any of the official or semiofficial literary reference works. Nevertheless, his novels, in their settings, descriptions, and problems, are clearly conditioned by his East German origin.

The action of Johnson's most successful novel, *Mutmaßungen über Jakob* (1959; Speculations about Jakob), takes place east of the Elbe. In fact, the book was written by Johnson while he was still living in East Germany. The general standards of the officially approved socialist novel are observed. It appears quite evident that Johnson hoped to have his novel published in East Germany.

The action begins in the fall of 1956. The hero, in accord with socialist requirements, is a poor but honest worker, the extremely loyal and conscientious railroad dispatcher Jakob Abs. The kindly, humane party functionary is also present, Captain Rohlfs of the Security Police. The vacillating, uncertain intellectual appears in the person of Jonas Blach, a technician at the East Berlin University.

The question of flight from East Germany, which is the central theme, is handled in the officially approved manner. Gesine Cresspahl, the chief female character of the novel, flees to the West, where she is obliged to engage in counterespionage. Jakob Abs, her friend, visits her. She begs him to stay with her in West Germany, but he refuses despite the fact that his mother has decided to remain there. Loyally he returns to East Germany.

All these elements, which conform with communist literary standards, would seem to make the novel entirely acceptable to the party. There are, however, serious undertones of protest, as well as a number of deviating stylistic factors that the sharp-eyed communist censors at once spotted. Basically, the aims of the party and the intentions of Johnson are far apart.

Johnson does not completely reject the socialist state. But he protests quite sharply against the simplified and false presentation of the life of the average citizen in East Germany and against the ideological determinism that controls all thought and action.

Johnson refuses to accept one of the basic theses of socialist realism; namely, that everything must be determined according to party criteria. He aims to be an unbiased reporter; he wants to be free to praise and to blame, to accuse and to glorify, on the basis of his own personal judgment. This, of course, is entirely contrary to the communist point of view, which denies the right of the individual to personal judgment.

The pervading tone and spirit of Johnson's novel is essentially opposed to socialist realism, which demands a clear separation of light and dark, an unequivocal answer to political and social questions, and the ignoring of all unsolved problems. Johnson is deliberately vague and diffuse; he creates an atmosphere of twilight. He presents contradictions and enigmas, doubt instead of certainty, search instead of solution.

Johnson's point of view is aptly brought out in the death of Jakob Abs, who, while trying to cross the rails, avoids a locomotive approaching from one direction but is run over by another coming from the opposite direction. He may have committed suicide, but this is not stated. The mere fact is that this just man, on familiar ground, is caught between two forces, one of which comes from East Germany and one from West Germany. A touch of irony is added by having two spies, a man from East Germany and the girl from West Germany, mourn the dead man who had rejected espionage.

In the sequel to *Mutmaßungen über Jakob*, that is, *Das dritte Buch über Achim* (1961; Third Book about Achim), written in West Germany, Johnson looks at a divided Germany from a new perspective. He protests against the superficial, prejudiced clichés of West German writers in their evaluation of East Germany. The central figure is a visitor from West Germany. Karsch, a journalist from Hamburg, visits East Germany in 1960. An East German publisher asks him to write a book about Achim, a popular cyclist. Karsch's research, his meetings with the athlete, and his arguments with the party functionaries who keep a close watch on his writing form the content of the novel.

Although Johnson's labyrinthine prose is at times difficult to follow, he has developed a style that allows him to express his attempt to grasp the present with epic means.

Johnson, whose roots are in the East and who is primarily concerned with the East German scene, has become one of the outstanding authors of West Germany.

Notes

Arnold Zweig

1. Marcel Reich-Ranicki, *Deutsche Literatur in West und Ost* (Munich: Piper & Co., 1965), p. 309.
2. Reich-Ranicki, *Deutsche Literatur*, pp. 311–12.
3. Reich-Ranicki, *Deutsche Literatur*, p. 332.

Hans Marchwitza

1. Marcel Reich-Ranicki, *Literarisches Leben in Deutschland* (Munich: Piper & Co., 1965), pp. 233–38.

Bertolt Brecht

1. Martin Esslin, *Brecht: the Man and His Work* (New York: Doubleday, 1960), p. 7.

2. H. R. Hays, *Bertolt Brecht: Selected Poems* (New York: Grove Press, 1947), pp. 4–5.
3. *Deutsche Literaturgeschichte* (Berlin: Volk und Wissen Volkseigener Verlag, 1965), p. 602.
4. Esslin, *Brecht,* pp. 30–31.
5. Esslin, *Brecht,* pp. 130–31.
6. Esslin, *Brecht,* pp. 139–42.
7. Esslin, *Brecht,* p. 269.

Anna Seghers

1. Marcel Reich-Ranicki, *Deutsche Literatur in West und Ost* (Munich: Piper & Co., 1965), pp. 357–58.
2. Reich-Ranicki, *Deutsche Literatur,* p. 361.
3. Reich-Ranicki, *Deutsche Literatur,* pp. 366–68.
4. Reich-Ranicki, *Deutsche Literatur,* p. 384.

Erwin Strittmatter

1. Marcel Reich-Ranicki, *Deutsche Literatur in West und Ost,* p. 421.

Bibliography

Histories of Literature and Criticism

Geerdts, H. J. *Deutsche Literaturgeschichte.* Berlin: Volk und Wissen Volkseigener Verlag, 1965.

Reich-Ranicki, Marcel. *Literarisches Leben in Deutschland.* Munich: Piper & Co., 1965.

————. *Deutsche Literatur in West und Ost.* Munich: Piper & Co., 1965.

Hatfield, Henry. *Modern German Literature.* New York: St. Martin's Press, 1967.

Anderle, Hans Peter. *Mitteldeutsche Erzähler.* Cologne: Verlag Wissenschaft und Politik, 1965.

Kunisch, Hermann, ed. *Handbuch der deutschen Gegenwartsliteratur.* Munich: Nymphenburger Verlagshandlung, 1965.

Esslin, Martin. *Brecht: the Man and His Work.* New York: Doubleday, 1960.

125

Ewen, Frederic. *Bertolt Brecht: His Life, His Art, and His Times.* New York: The Citadel Press, 1970.

Anthologies

PROSE

Im Licht des Jahrhunderts: Deutsche Erzähler unserer Zeit. Berlin: Verlag der Nation, 1964.

Anderle, Hans Peter. *Mitteldeutsche Erzähler.* Cologne: Verlag Wissenschaft und Politik, 1965.

POETRY

Deutsche Lyrik auf der anderen Seite. Munich: Carl Hanser Verlag, 1960.

Biography

Pädagogisches Institut Leipzig, Abteilung Deutschunterricht für Ausländer. *Schriftsteller der DDR.* Leipzig, 1968.

————. *Lexikon deutschsprachiger Schriftsteller von den Anfängen bis zur Gegenwart.* 2 vols. Leipzig, 1967, 1968.

Index

127